U.S. Fish & Wildlife Service

Comprehensive Conservation Plan

Ninigret National Wildlife Refuge

Prepared by:

Nancy McGarigal, Refuge Planner
Northeast Regional Office, Division of Planning
300 Westgate Center Drive
Hadley, MA 01035
(413) 253-8562

Local contact:

Charlie Vandemoer, Refuge Manager
3769 D Old Post Road
Charlestown, RI 02813
(401) 364-9124

Cover photo: Spring peeper, USFWS photo

May 2002

*This goose, designed by J.N. `Ding"
Darling, has become a symbol of the
National Wildlife Refuge System.*

The *U.S. Fish & Wildlife Service* is the principal federal agency responsible for conserving, protecting, and enhancing fish and wildlife and their habitats for the continuing benefit of the American people. The Service manages the 93-million acre National Wildlife Refuge System comprised of more than 500 national wildlife refuges and thousands of waterfowl production areas. It also operates 66 national fish hatcheries and 78 ecological services field stations. The agency enforces federal wildlife laws, manages migratory bird populations, restores nationally significant fisheries, conserves and restores wildlife habitat such as wetlands, administers the Endangered Species Act, and helps foreign governments with their conservation efforts. It also oversees the Federal Aid program which distributes hundreds of millions of dollars in excise taxes on fishing and hunting equipment to state wildlife agencies.

Comprehensive Conservation Plans provide long term guidance for management decisions; set forth goals, objectives, and strategies needed to accomplish refuge purposes; and, identify the Service's best estimate of future needs. These plans detail program planning levels that are sometimes substantially above current budget allocations and, as such, are primarily for Service strategic planning and program prioritization purposes. The plans do not constitute a commitment for staffing increases, operational and maintenance increases, or funding for future land acquisition.

Comprehensive Conservation Plan Approval
for Ninigret National Wildlife Refuge

Submitted by:

[signature]   6/21/02
Charles E. Vandemoer,   Date
Refuge Manager,
Rhode Island NWR Complex

Approved by:

[signature]   7/16/02
Richard W. Dyer,   Date
Refuge Supervisor, North
National Wildlife Refuge System

Approved by:

[signature]   8/9/02
Anthony D. Léger,   Date
Northeast Regional Chief,
National Wildlife Refuge System

Final approval:

[signature]   8/13/02
Dr. Mamie A. Parker,   Date
Regional Director, Region 5
U.S. Fish and Wildlife Service

Table of Contents
Ninigret National Wildlife Refuge CCP

Chapter 1

Native bluestemgrass
USFWS photo

Introduction and Background

- Refuge Overview
- Purpose of and Need for a CCP
- Mission
- Refuge Purpose
- National and Regional Mandates Guiding this CCP
- Existing Partnerships

Introduction

This Comprehensive Conservation Plan (CCP) is the culmination of a planning process that began in February 1998. Numerous meetings with the public, the state, and conservation partners were held to identify and evaluate management alternatives. A draft Comprehensive Conservation Plan and Environmental Assessment (CCP/EA) was distributed in December 2000. This CCP presents the management goals, objectives, and strategies that we believe will best achieve our vision for the refuge, contribute to the National Wildlife Refuge System Mission, achieve refuge purposes and legal mandates, and serve the American public.

Refuge Overview

Ninigret Refuge is located in Charlestown, Rhode Island, 30 miles south of Providence (see maps 1-1 and 1-2). Transfers of land from the U.S. Navy to the Service primarily established and expanded the refuge, including: 27.5 acres of the Ninigret Pond barrier beach in 1970, 316.4 acres of the Naval Landing Field in 1979, and an additional 60 acres 1982. With the recent acquisition of two large tracts of mature deciduous forest north of U.S. Route 1, the refuge now owns 701 acres. There are 390 unacquired acres within the newly expanded refuge acquisition boundary (see Appendix E, Land Protection Plan).

Ninigret Refuge is composed of a mainland parcel and a barrier beach parcel. Its mainland parcel contains 674 acres, including 3 miles of shoreline on Ninigret Pond. The barrier beach parcel contains 27.5 acres between Ninigret Pond and Block Island Sound.

The Purpose of and Need for a CCP

Developing a CCP is vital to refuge management. The purpose of the CCP is to provide strategic management direction over the next 15 years, by...

- Providing a clear statement of desired future conditions for habitat, wildlife, visitor services, and facilities;
- Providing refuge neighbors, visitors, and partners with a clear understanding of the reasons for management actions;
- Ensuring refuge management reflects the policies and goals of the Refuge System and legal mandates;
- Ensuring the compatibility of current and future public use;
- Providing long-term continuity and direction for refuge management; and
- Providing direction for staffing, operations, maintenance, and developing budget requests.

The need to develop a CCP for Ninigret Refuge is two-fold. First, the 1997 National Wildlife Refuge System Improvement Act (Refuge Improvement Act) requires that all national wildlife refuges have a CCP in place by 2012 to help fulfill the mission of the Refuge System. Second, the refuge lacks a master plan that establishes priorities and ensures consistent, integrated management among the five refuges in the Rhode Island Refuge Complex.

Map 1-1

Rhode Island National Wildlife Refuge Complex
U.S. Fish & Wildlife Service Current Ownership

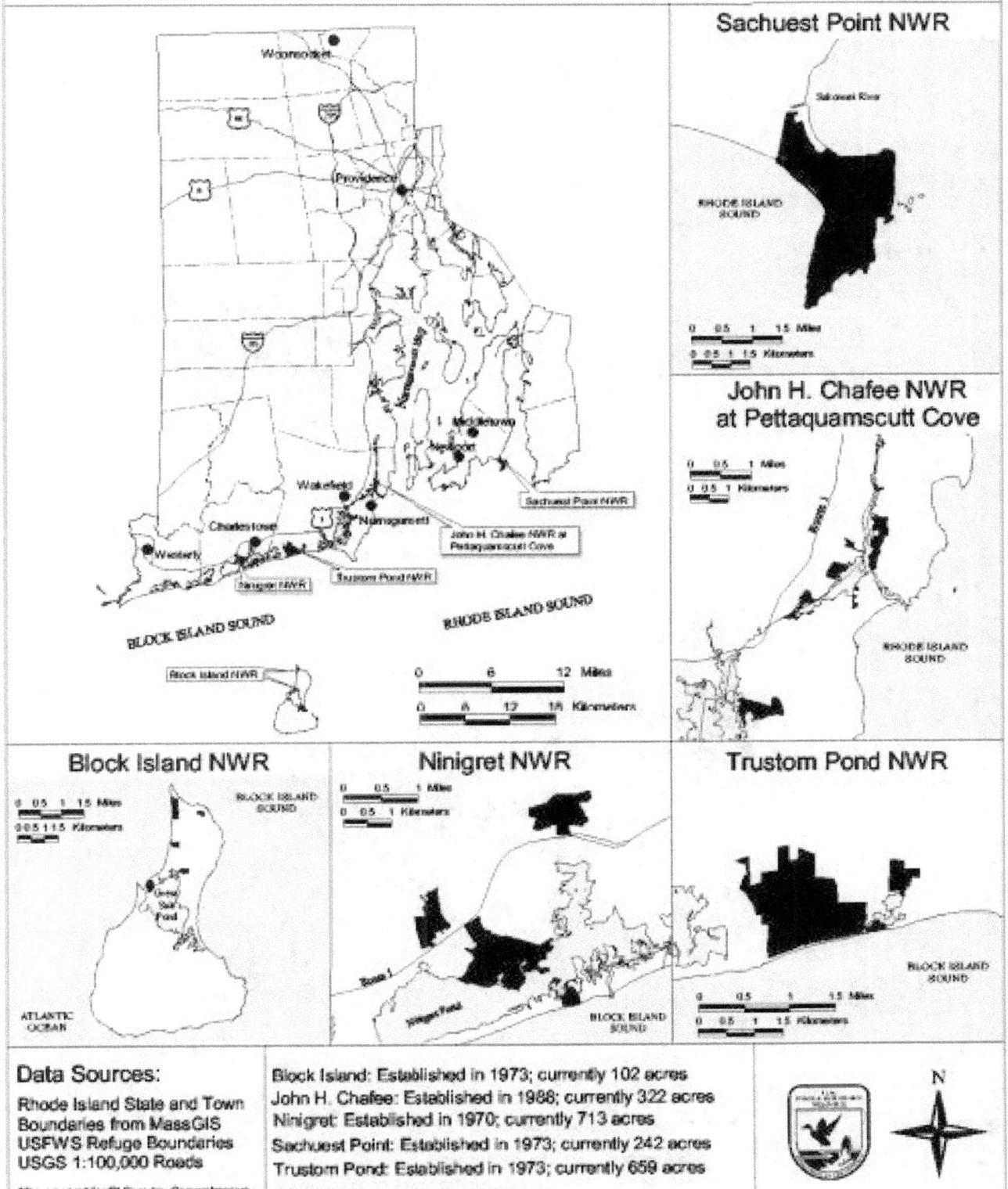

Data Sources:

Rhode Island State and Town
Boundaries from MassGIS
USFWS Refuge Boundaries
USGS 1:100,000 Roads

Map prepared for RI Complex Comprehensive
Conservation Plan, March 2002

Block Island: Established in 1973; currently 102 acres
John H. Chafee: Established in 1988; currently 322 acres
Ninigret: Established in 1970; currently 713 acres
Sachuest Point: Established in 1973; currently 242 acres
Trustom Pond: Established in 1973; currently 659 acres

*Acreage figures are approximate.

Map 1-2

Ninigret National Wildlife Refuge
Current Ownership and Approved Acquisition Boundary
Rhode Island NWR Complex Comprehensive Conservation Plan

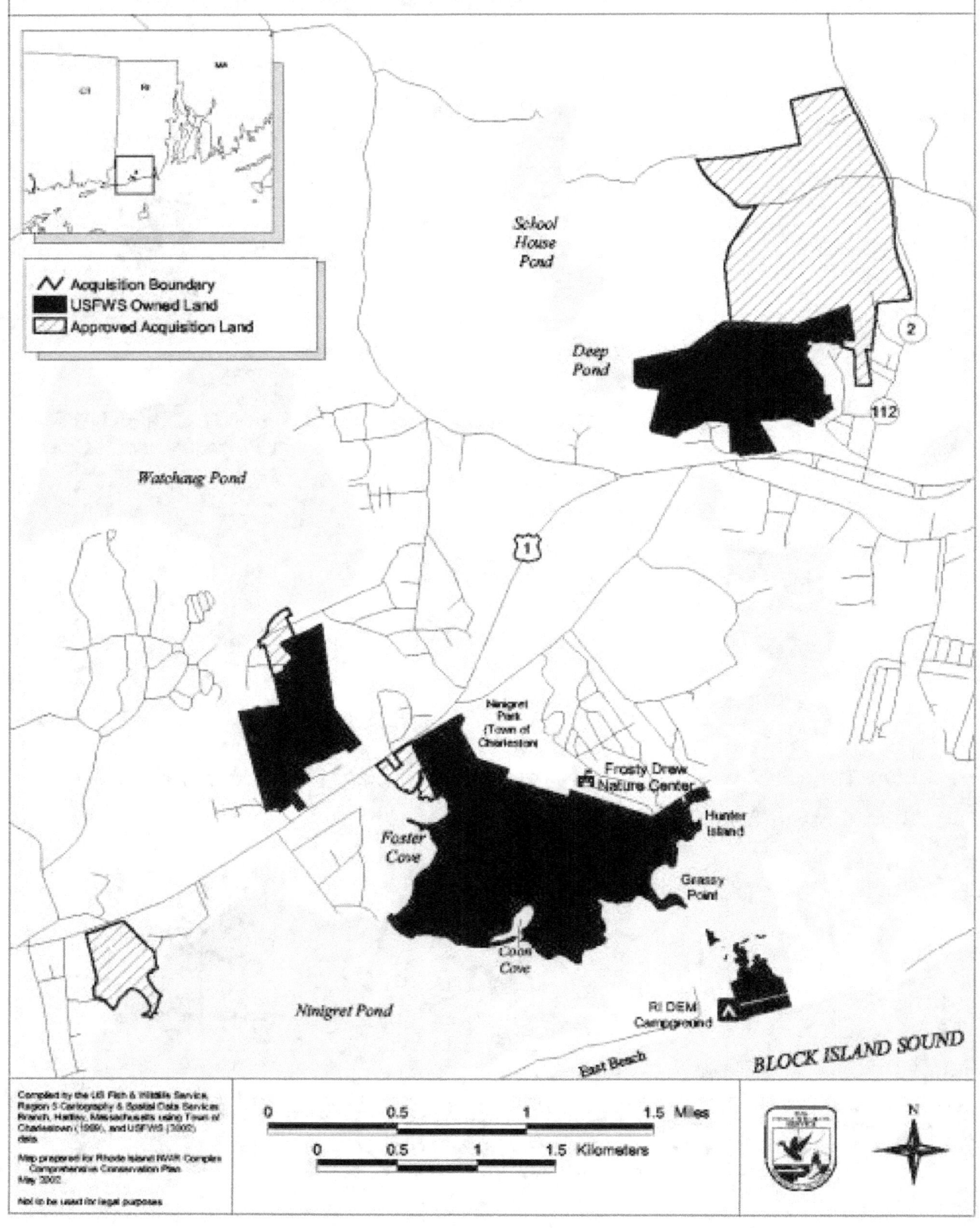

Acquisition Boundary
USFWS Owned Land
Approved Acquisition Land

School House Pond

Deep Pond

Watchaug Pond

Ninigret Park (Town of Charlestown)

Frosty Drew Nature Center

Hunter Island

Foster Cove

Grassy Point

Coon Cove

Ninigret Pond

RI DEM Campground

East Beach

BLOCK ISLAND SOUND

Compiled by the US Fish & Wildlife Service, Region 5 Cartography & Spatial Data Services Branch, Hadley, Massachusetts using Town of Charlestown (1999), and USFWS (2000) data.

Map prepared for Rhode Island NWR Complex Comprehensive Conservation Plan. May 2002.

Not to be used for legal purposes.

0   0.5   1   1.5 Miles
0   0.5   1   1.5 Kilometers

N

The U.S. Fish and Wildlife Service and its Mission

"...working with others, to conserve, protect and enhance fish wildlife, and plants and their habitats for the continuing benefit of the American people."

– Mission, U.S. Fish & Wildlife Service

The Service, part of the Department of the Interior, manages national wildlife refuges and national fish hatcheries. By law, Congress entrusts national resources to the Service for conservation and protection: migratory birds and fish, endangered species, inter-jurisdictional fish, wetlands, and certain marine mammals. The Service also enforces federal wildlife laws and international treaties on importing and exporting wildlife, assists with state fish and wildlife programs, and helps other countries develop wildlife conservation programs.

The National Wildlife Refuge System and its Mission

The Refuge System is the world's largest collection of lands and waters set aside specifically for conserving wildlife and protecting ecosystems. More than 525 national wildlife refuges, in every state and a number of U.S. Territories, protect more than 93 million acres. More than 34 million visitors annually hunt, fish, observe and photograph wildlife, or participate in environmental education and interpretive activities on refuges.

"...to administer a national network of lands and waters for the conservation, management, and where appropriate, restoration of the fish, wildlife, and plant resources and their habitats within the United States for the benefit of present and future generations of Americans."

– Refuge System Mission, Refuge Improvement Act; Public Law 105-57

In 1997, Congress passed the National Wildlife Refuge System Improvement Act, establishing a unifying mission for the Refuge System, and a new process for determining compatible public use activities on refuges. It also requires that we prepare a CCP for each refuge. The act states that, first and foremost, the Refuge System must focus on wildlife conservation. It further states that the mission of the Refuge System, coupled with the purpose(s) for which each refuge was established, will provide management direction for each refuge.

On public use, the act declares that all existing or proposed public uses must be compatible with each refuge's purpose. It highlights six wildlife-dependent public uses as priorities that all CCPs must evaluate: environmental education and interpretation, fishing, hunting, and wildlife observation and photography. Each refuge manager determines the compatibility of an activity by evaluating its potential impact on refuge resources, insuring that the activity supports the Refuge System mission, and ensuring that the activity does not materially detract from or interfere with the refuge purpose.

Refuge Purposes

The establishment purposes for Ninigret Refuge are:

"... for use as an inviolate sanctuary, or for any other management purpose, for migratory birds,"

– Migratory Bird Conservation Act of 1929

"... particular value in carrying out the national migratory bird management program"

– Transfer of Certain Real Property for Conservation Purposes Act of 1972

National and Regional Mandates Guiding this Project

This section highlights Service policy, legal mandates, and existing resource plans, arranged from the national to the local level, that directly influenced development of this CCP.

The *Digest of Federal Resource Laws of Interest to the USFWS* lists the various federal laws, Executive Orders, treaties, interstate compacts, and regulations on conserving and protecting natural and cultural resources (online at http://laws.fws.gov/lawsdigest/indx.html). The Service Manual and Refuge Manual contain Service policies and guidance on planning and day-to-day refuge management. The draft CCP/EA was written to fulfill compliance with NEPA.

North American Waterfowl Management Plan (May 14, 1986)

This plan outlines the strategy among the United States, Canada, and Mexico to restore waterfowl populations by protecting, restoring, and enhancing habitat within 11 U.S. Joint Venture Areas and three species Joint Ventures: Arctic Goose, Black Duck, and Sea Duck. Partnerships among federal, state and provincial governments, tribal nations, local businesses, conservation organizations, and individual citizens protect that habitat. The Refuge Complex lies within the Atlantic Coast Joint Venture, which has identified 13 priority focus areas totaling 3,226 acres of both wetlands and adjacent uplands for protection in Rhode Island (Atlantic Coast Joint Venture 1988). Three priority focus areas in the Refuge Complex are Trustom Pond, Ninigret Pond, and the Pettaquamscutt (Narrow) River.

Black duck. *USFWS photo.*

Since black ducks winter in Rhode Island, the goals and objectives of the Black Duck Joint Venture apply to managing the Refuge Complex. The Black Duck Joint Venture has identified the coastal salt marsh habitats along the mid-upper Atlantic coast as important wintering habitat.

Partners in Flight Landbird Conservation Plan: Physiographic Area 9, Southern New England (draft, October 2000)

In 1990, Partners in Flight (PIF) was conceived as a voluntary, international coalition of government agencies, conservation organizations, academic institutions, private industry, and other citizens dedicated to reversing the downward trends of declining species and "keeping common birds common." The foundation of PIF's long-term strategy for bird conservation is a series of scientifically based Landbird Conservation Plans. The goal of each PIF Landbird Conservation Plan is to ensure long term maintenance of healthy populations of native landbirds.

The PIF Program is developing a plan for the Southern New England Physiographic Area, using existing data on habitat loss, landbird population trends, and the vulnerability of species and habitats to threats, to rank the conservation priority of landbird species. The plan will identify focal species for each habitat type from which population and habitat objectives and conservation actions will be determined. We utilized this draft document for the list of priority species to consider in management. A revised draft of the plan was released in October 2000, and we will use the final plan, when finished, to further guide management.

Connecticut River/Long Island Sound Ecosystem Priorities, 1997

During the last decade, we have emphasized ecosystem conservation, particularly the role of refuges within ecosystems, and their ability to affect the long-term conservation of natural resources. Implementing an ecosystem approach to resource management is one of our top national priorities. We have initiated new partnerships with private landowners, state and federal agencies, corporations, conservation groups, and volunteers, to form 52 ecosystem teams across the country, typically using large river watersheds to define ecosystems. Those teams work on developing goals and priorities for research and management within each ecosystem.

The Refuge Complex lies within our Connecticut River/Long Island Sound Ecosystem (Map 1-3). A team composed of Fish and Wildlife Service personnel and representatives from six State Fish and Wildlife Departments developed a Priority Resources Plan (July 1996) that identifies seven priorities, each involving numerous action strategies.

1. Protect, restore, and enhance listed and candidate populations...with special emphasis on beach strand species, coastal sandplain habitat, and Connecticut River species.

2. Protect, restore, and enhance anadromous and interjurisdictional migratory fish populations...with special emphasis on Atlantic salmon, American shad, shortnose sturgeon, and river herring.

3. Reverse the decline of migrant landbirds...with special emphasis on grassland and forest interior species.

4. Protect, restore, and enhance populations of colonial nesting waterbirds, shorebirds, and waterfowl...with special emphasis on coastal areas and major rivers.

5. Protect, restore, and enhance wetland habitats.

6. Manage refuge lands to protect, restore, and enhance native communities and trust resources.

7. Develop a public that values the fish and wildlife resources...understands events and issues related to these resources, and acts to promote fish and wildlife conservation.

Northeast Areas Study: Significant Coastal Habitats of Southern New England And Portions of Long Island, New York (USFWS 1991)

Recognizing the biological and economic importance of the coast's living resources and natural values to the region and the Nation, in 1990 Congress funded a study to identify coastal areas in southern New England and Long Island whose fish and wildlife habitat need protection and whose natural diversity needs preservation. The Northeast Coastal Study identifies species of regional importance, and describes regionally significant habitat complexes. It specifically describes significant or unique habitat, threats to sustaining the habitat complex, and considerations for conserving and protecting it. We utilized this study in the development of our land protection strategies.

Map 1-3

Connecticut River/Long Island Sound Ecosystem
Comprehensive Conservation Plan

CANADA

ME

VT

NH

Conte-Nulhegan Basin Division

John Hay NWR

NY

Silvio O. Conte NF&WR

MA

CT

RI

Ninigret NWR

Trustom Pond NWR

John H. Chafee NWR

Sachuest Point NWR

Monomoy NWR

Mashpee NWR

Nantucket NWR

Stewart B. McKinney NWR

Block Island Sound

Block Island NWR

Nomans Land Island NWR

Long Island Sound

Elizabeth A. Morton NWR

Target Rock NWR

ATLANTIC OCEAN

Data Sources:

USGS 1:2,000,000 Hydrography & States.
All other data provided by USFWS & So.
New England/NY Bight Coastal Program.

Map prepared for Rhode Island NWR Complex
Comprehensive Conservation Plan
June 2002
Not to be used for legal purposes.

| 0 | 40 | 80 | 120 | Miles |

| 0 | 60 | 120 | 180 | Kilometers |

N

The study identifies these habitat complexes in Rhode Island:

1. Fishers Island Sound (located in Suffolk and New London Counties, CT, and Washington County, RI)

2. Chapman Swamp/Pawcatuck River (Washington County, RI)

3. Maschaug Pond and Beach (Washington County, RI)

Piping Plover (Charadrius melodus), Atlantic Coast Population, Revised Recovery Plan, 1996

The piping plover is the only federally-listed endangered or threatened species that currently breeds on refuge lands within the Rhode Island Refuge Complex. The primary objective of the revised recovery program is to remove the Atlantic coast piping plover population from the List of Endangered and Threatened Wildlife and Plants by:

■ Achieving well-distributed increases in numbers and productivity of breeding pairs; and

■ Providing for long-term protection of breeding and wintering plovers and their habitats.

The Revised Recovery Plan describes detailed "Recovery Tasks" needed to meet the recovery objective. The Rhode Island Refuge Complex is specifically mentioned in the following tasks:

■ Draw down or create coastal ponds where feasible to make more feeding habitat available.

■ Reduce disturbance of breeding plovers from humans and pets.

■ Develop mechanisms to provide long-term protection of plovers and their habitat.

The Recovery Plan incorporates management guidelines for recreational activities in piping plover breeding habitat, which were developed by our Ecological Services Division in 1994. While not regulatory, these recommendations continue to serve as our best professional advice for complying with the Endangered Species Act. We utilized these same guidelines in developing management actions.

Regional Wetlands Concept Plan – Emergency Wetlands Resources Act 9 (USFWS 1990)

In 1986, Congress enacted the Emergency Wetlands Resources Act to promote the conservation of our nation's wetlands. The Act directed the Department of Interior to develop a National Wetlands Priority Conservation Plan identifying the location and types of wetlands that should receive priority for acquisition by federal and state agencies using Land and Water Conservation Fund appropriations. In 1990, the Service's Northeast Region completed a Regional Wetlands Concept Plan identifying a total of 850 wetland sites in the Region warranting consideration for acquisition due to wetland values. Wetland values, functions, and potential threats for each site were cited; 24 sites within the State of Rhode Island were listed.

**Protecting Our Land Resources:
A Land Acquisition and Protection Plan, Rhode Island Department
of Environmental Management, May 1996**

The purpose of this State plan is to assist agencies within the Rhode
Island Department of Environmental Management (RI DEM) in
protecting land to support their primary mission, "...protection of
the integrity of natural resources essential to the environmental,
economic and social welfare of the citizens of Rhode Island." Its
framework provides strategies to permanently protect five critical
State resources: agriculture, forestry, drinking water, recreation, and
natural heritage and biodiversity. It includes evaluation criteria for
selecting and prioritizing lands.

Special Area Management Plan – Salt Pond Region, November 1998

This plan details management strategies for implementing the
program standards of the State of Rhode Island Coastal Resources
Management Council (CRMC) in the Salt Pond Region. The Salt
Pond Region SAMP includes eight objectives; the following six relate
to Ninigret Refuge:

1. To maintain the exceptional scenic qualities of the Salt Pond
   Region, and a diversity in the mix and intensity of the activities
   they support.

2. To prevent expansion near areas of the salt ponds that are
   contaminated by potentially harmful bacteria or eutrophic
   conditions.

3. To ensure the groundwater will be unpolluted.

4. To preserve and enhance the diversity and abundance of fish and
   shellfish.

5. To restore the barrier beaches, salt marshes, and fish and wildlife
   habitats damaged by past construction or present use.

6. To create a decision-making process appropriate to the
   management of the region as an ecosystem.

Existing partnerships

Throughout this CCP, we use the term "partners". In addition to our volunteers, we receive significant help from the following partners:

- Southern New England/New York Bight Coastal Ecosystems Office (FWS)
- Ecological Services, New England Field Office (FWS)
- Friends of the National Wildlife Refuges of Rhode Island
- Rhode Island Department of Environmental Management (RI DEM)
- The Nature Conservancy, Rhode Island and Block Island Offices
- University of Rhode Island, Department of Natural Resources Science (URI)
- Audubon Society of Rhode Island
- Rhode Island Coastal Resources Management Council (RI CRMC)
- Local land trusts
- Narragansett Indian Tribal Council
- Frosty Drew Nature Center

Chapter 2

Public Open House on CCP, Rhode Island
USFWS photo

Planning Process

- The Comprehensive Conservation Planning Process
- Issues, Concerns, and Opportunities

The Comprehensive Conservation Planning Process

Given the mandate in the Refuge Improvement Act to develop a CCP for each national wildlife refuge, our Northeast Regional Office began the planning process for the Rhode Island Refuge Complex in February 1998. Figure 2-1 displays the steps of the planning process and how they incorporate National Environmental Policy Act (NEPA) requirements.

First, we focused on collecting information on natural resources and public use at the Refuge Complex, and developed its long-term vision and preliminary goals, including issues associated with each of its refuges. Next, we compiled a mailing list of more than 2,000 organizations and individuals, to ensure we would be contacting a diverse sample of the interested public.

Recognizing that not everyone could attend the Open Houses planned for April and May 1998, we developed Issues Workbooks in March to encourage even more people to provide their written comments on topics related to managing the Refuge Complex. We offered the workbooks to everyone on our mailing list, including adjacent landowners, and made workbooks available at refuge headquarters, local libraries, and on the Internet from the Region 5 Home Page (http://www.northeast.fws.gov). We received 150 completed workbooks. Those responses and public input at our meetings have influenced our formulating issues and developing alternatives on resource protection and public use.

Figure 2-1. *NEPA and the CCP Process*

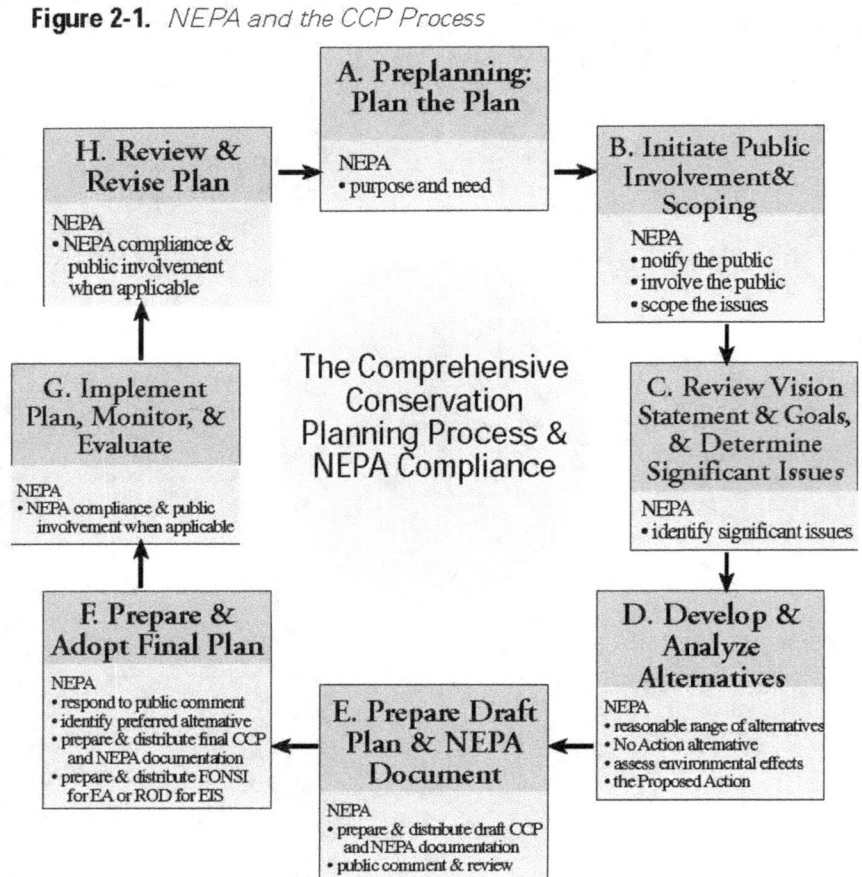

In April and May 1998, we began a series of public meetings: five Open Houses in the communities of Middletown, South Kingstown, Charlestown, and Block Island invited public comments on goals and issues. We advertised the meetings through news releases, radio broadcasts, and notices to our mailing list. From 15 to 40 people attended each meeting. We also organized 15 informational meetings with state and federal agencies, non-profit conservation groups, town planners, conservation commissions, and sporting clubs.

Public responses suggested more than 50 additional areas where lands warranted protection, typically along the coast. We evaluated those lands for their potential as national wildlife refuges, using criteria such as the presence of threatened, endangered, or other trust species and their habitats, the presence of wetlands, our ability to manage or restore the areas, existing threats to their integrity, and their size and location.

We distributed a Planning Update to everyone on our mailing list in September 1998. This newsletter summarized public comments from meetings and workbooks, described policy guidelines for managing public use on refuges, and identified the long-term vision and goals for the Refuge Complex.

Once the key issues had firmed up, we developed alternative strategies by May 1999 to resolve each one. We derived the strategies from public comment, follow-up contacts with partners, and ideas from the planning team. We distributed a second Planning Update newsletter in May 1999, updating everyone on our planning timelines and our decision to start a separate Environmental Assessment for the visitor center/headquarters.

We released a draft CCP/EA in December of 2000 for a 51-day comment period. We held public hearings and open houses in February of 2001. A summary of public comments is included in Appendix B. The land acquisition component of this planning process is contained in the Land Protection Plan (Appendix E).

Each year, we will evaluate our accomplishments under this CCP, including the completion of more detailed step down plans. Monitoring or new information results may indicate the need to change our strategies. We will modify the CCP documents and associated management activities as needed, following the procedures outlined in Service policy and NEPA requirements. This CCP will be fully revised every 15 years, or sooner if necessary.

Issues, Concerns, and Opportunities

From the Issues Workbooks, public and focus group meetings, and planning team discussions, we developed a list of issues, concerns, opportunities, or any other items requiring a management decision. Then we sorted them into two categories: "Key issues," and "Issues and concerns considered outside the scope of this analysis".

Key issues, along with goals, formed the basis for developing and comparing the different management alternatives in the draft CCP/EA.

Issues and concerns outside the scope of this analysis were discussed in the draft CCP/EA but will not be addressed futher in this final CCP.

Key Issues

Public and partner meetings and further team discussions produced the key issues briefly described below.

1. Protection of endangered and threatened species and other species and habitats of special concern.

This is the most important issue facing the Refuge Complex. Protecting federally listed endangered and threatened species is integral to the mission of the Refuge System, and is a common purpose for which each of the five refuges was established. Other federal trust species are also of primary concern, including migratory birds, anadromous fish, and certain marine mammals.

In the forefront of this issue is management for piping plover, a federally listed species (threatened). Piping plover nest on the beaches at Trustom Pond Refuge and Ninigret Refuge, and on the Narrow River estuary near Chafee Refuge. Block Island Refuge has potential nesting habitat; so far, nesting attempts there have been unsuccessful.

Threats from coastal development, disturbance by humans and pets, and predation are the major factors contributing to the species decline (Piping Plover Atlantic Coast Population, Revised Recovery Plan, 1996). Protecting piping plover presently requires an intensive effort by refuge staff who monitor plover nesting, manage public use and access on beaches, control predators at nest sites, and provide environmental education and interpretation about the natural history of piping plover and barrier beach protection.

Consistently each year, predators are one of the most significant factors affecting chick survival in Rhode Island. Also, since 1993, humans have caused three incidents of piping plover nest destruction: two were acts of vandalism directed at destroying nests and eggs; the third may have resulted from joyriding on the beach. Campers often leave trash, which attracts predators to a nesting area, and often unleash their dogs, who chase adult plover off nests.

Some responses raised the continuing issue of restricting public beach use. Some feel we could do more to provide for piping plover by restoring habitat, or by working with the Rhode Island Coastal Resources Management Council (CRMC) to close beach intertidal areas.

Service staff help coordinate piping plover monitoring on nine beaches in southern Rhode Island, as well as on the refuges. This requires tremendous time and resources, both presently limited. Funding for plover work along the South Shore is inconsistent from year to year, and totally dependent on non-Service funding sources, typically foundation grants. However, the benefits derived are clearly evident in increased nesting attempts and productivity on many sites.

Other federally listed species discussed are the seabeach amaranth (threatened), and sandplain gerardia (endangered), two plant species that may be considered for future reintroduction. Current levels of refuge management also emphasize other federal trust resources: Neotropical migratory birds, waterfowl, and colonial wading birds.

Appendix A lists species and habitats of special management concern. That list includes the status of all plants, wildlife, fish, and rare natural communities known to occur in Rhode Island that are federally listed as endangered or threatened, were candidates for listing, or are otherwise of management concern. Combined with location information, we used that list to identify additional land protection needs and opportunities. We know very little about many of these species' presence on or use of refuge habitats. The alternatives in the draft CCP/EA differed in their strategies for managing these species and habitats. Addressing this issue will help achieve Goal 1: Protect and enhance federal trust resources and other species and habitats of special concern.

2. Restoration and maintenance of coastal sandplain and maritime natural communities, including grasslands and shrublands (less than 60 years old).

While it is true that the Northeast landscape was primarily forested prior to rapid agricultural settlement in the 1800's, grasslands quickly became a dominant part of the landscape in the 19th century. Grassland-dependent species responded in kind and became established. Over the last several decades, however, coastal sandplain grasslands and shrublands, coastal maritime grasslands and shrublands, and agricultural fields and pastures, have been in rapid decline in New England due to a combination of development, changes in agricultural technology, succession to forest as farms were abandoned, and lack of a natural disturbance such as fire (Vickery 1997).

In Rhode Island, the State's farmland dropped nearly 50 percent between 1964 and 1997, from 103,801 to 55,256 acres. An additional 3,100 acres of farmland will be lost in the next 20 years if current sprawl patterns continue (Common Ground 2000). As a result, few large, contiguous grasslands and shrublands are left; only smaller, fragmented, and isolated habitat patches remain (< 75 acres).

These smaller areas are unsuitable for many focus species, including once-common grassland birds such as grasshopper sparrow and upland sandpiper. Grasshopper sparrows have declined by 69 percent in the past 25 years, according to Breeding Bird Survey data (Vickery 1997). Our best available information suggests that grasslands should ideally be managed in 100 acre or larger patches. Smaller grassland habitat patches are much less productive for grassland birds, and could serve as "sinks", where species try to nest, but because of increased predation and other factors, productivity and survival is severly limited.

Other grassland and shrubland species have declined dramatically as well. Many of Rhode Island's State-listed plant and animal species are dependent on these habitat types.

Tremendous potential exists for refuge staff to become involved in restoring habitat on private lands. Grassland and shrubland restoration offers opportunities for our staff to provide technical expertise to local communities. The alternatives in the draft CCP/EA compared different levels of restoring and maintaining these habitats and providing technical assistance to private landowners. Addressing this issue will help achieve Goal 2: Maintain and/or restore natural ecological communities to promote healthy, functioning ecosystems.

3. Protection and restoration of the beach strand ecological community.

Beach strand habitat is in critically short supply due to its loss and degradation by development and shoreline de-stabilization. Meanwhile, the demand for recreational uses in these areas intensifies. The result is an alarmingly high rate of habitat loss and the decline of virtually all beach strand plant and animal species. Federally listed species such as the piping plover, roseate tern, northeastern beach tiger beetle, and seabeach amaranth depend on this habitat. Alternatives in the draft CCP/EA included different strategies for protecting it. Addressing this issue will help achieve Goal 2: Maintain and/or restore natural ecological communities to promote healthy, functioning ecosystems.

4. Protection and restoration of wetlands.

The well documented values of healthy wetlands include fish and wildlife habitat, flood protection, erosion control, and water quality maintenance. Despite laws and regulations to protect them, wetlands throughout Rhode Island have been rapidly declining since the 1960's through conversion to agriculture, residential and industrial development. Rhode Island has developed more land in the last 34 years than in its first 325 years (Common Ground May/June 2000). Most recent sprawl occurs outside the urban areas, near the remaining wetlands.

Estuarine wetlands consisting of tidal salt and brackish waters are of particular concern. Invasive species are dominating refuge wetlands and threatening their biodiversity.

Non-point pollution and sources off-refuge are impacting water quality and the health and productivity of these wetlands. The alternatives in the draft CCP/EA included different levels of management for restoring wetlands and for cooperatively managing entire watersheds. Addressing this issue will help achieve Goal 2: Maintain and/or restore natural ecological communities to promote healthy, functioning ecosystems.

5. Control of invasive, non-native, or overabundant plant and wildlife species.

Each of the five refuges has an extensive distribution of invasive plant species. These plants are a threat because they displace native plant and animal species, degrade wetlands and other natural communities, and reduce natural diversity and wildlife habitat values. They outcompete native species by dominating light, water, and nutrient resources. Once established, getting rid of invasive plants is expensive and labor-intensive. Unfortunately, their characteristic abilities to establish easily, reproduce prolifically, and disperse readily, make eradication difficult. Many of these plants cause measurable economic impacts, particularly in agricultural fields. Preventing new invasions is extremely important for maintaining biodiversity and native plant populations. The control of existing, affected areas will require extensive partnerships with adjacent landowners, state, and local governments.

Thirteen invasive plant species affecting the natural communities within the Refuge Complex are considered of high management concern. The most prevalent are *Phragmites*, purple loosestrife, Asian bittersweet, autumn olive, and Japanese honeysuckle. Other species such as Japanese knotweed and multiflora rose are increasing on the Refuge Complex, and likely to become an issue soon.

Several wildlife species occur on the Refuge Complex that are known, or suspected to be, adversely affecting natural diversity. Issues surface when these species directly impact federal trust species or degrade natural communities. Mute swans are non-native, invasive species that aggressively drive native waterfowl and shorebirds away from nesting areas, compete with them for food, degrade water quality when they spend extended periods of time molting on coastal ponds, and are sometimes aggressive towards humans.

Native species such as deer, red fox, gull, and small predatory mammals such as mink, skunk, and weasel can be a problem when their populations exceed the range of natural fluctuation and the ability of the habitat to support them. Excessive numbers of deer are a threat to rare plant communities on the Refuge Complex, and excessive browse lines are evident on two refuges. Adjacent landowners are also concerned about deer impacts on landscaping, the increase in vehicle-deer collisions, and the threat of Lyme disease.

Red fox, gull, and some small mammals are voracious predators that can adversely impact other native wildlife populations. Occurrences have been documented of herring and black-backed gull, red fox, and weasel preying on piping plover and least tern, a State-listed species (threatened). Fox easily habituate to humans, and were being hand-fed at Sachuest Point Refuge. Many people fear fox and other mammals because they can carry rabies. These predators are particularly troublesome when their populations exceed natural levels. Control measures for each species are controversial, and may include lethal removal, visual and audio deterrents, or destroying eggs, nests, or den sites.

The alternatives in the draft CCP/EA compared different strategies for managing invasive species. Addressing this issue will help achieve Goal 1: Protect and enhance Federal trust resources and other species and habitats of special concern, and Goal 2: Maintain and/or restore natural ecological communities to promote healthy, functioning ecosystems.

6. Protection of biologically significant areas through acquisition and/or cooperative management.

Public meetings, partner meetings, and workbook responses expressed a great deal of support for the protection of additional fish and wildlife habitat in southern Rhode Island. That support runs across the State, as Rhode Islanders consistently vote ballot measures to maintain open space and protect fish and wildlife habitats. Many people mentioned that their support stems from their concern over the rapid pace of development on the South Shore. As we stated earlier, development in non-urban areas of Rhode Island has increased dramatically over the last 30 years. It is now the second most densely populated State in the country. One estimate predicts that current sprawl patterns will ensure the loss of all its rural areas before 2100 (Common Ground 2000). The Rhode Island Office of The Nature Conservancy has noted that the conservation actions taken during the next 5 to 10 years will be the most important for the majority of Rhode Island towns (The Nature Conservancy 2000).

This dramatic increase in development has changed land use patterns and practices, significantly modifying natural landscapes. As natural lands (those with sustainable native species populations and intact ecological processes) become isolated and fragmented into smaller pieces disconnected from other natural areas, their ability to support a full complement of native species is adversely affected. Cut off from larger populations, species and plant communities within these natural areas face the problems of limited genetic exchange, a decreased ability to support diverse populations, and lost capacity to recruit new individuals. Ultimately, the number of native species declines and exotic species gain a stronghold. It is precisely this diminished ability of natural areas to support diverse species with different habitat requirements that leads to a decline in biodiversity. While some species can tolerate fragmentation as they prefer "edge habitat," many others, including "interior" dependent species, require larger, contiguous natural areas or functional corridors linking patches of natural habitat. This ability to protect and sustain larger natural areas and corridors, coupled with the protection of unique or rare species or communities, is critical to maintaining biodiversity.

A landscape or ecosystem approach to protecting land is also critical in the recovery of threatened and endangered species. Piping plover serve to illustrate this point. They have a fairly strong fidelity to certain nesting areas and typically return to them most years. Shifting of pairs between nesting areas has been observed when disturbances or habitat conditions affect their ability to nest. Barrier beaches are dynamic ecosystems, and their nesting conditions can change dramatically from year to year. While 1999 was a good nesting year on Moonstone Beach (Trustom Pond Refuge), in 2000, the beach consisted entirely of cobble with virtually no sand for nesting. The piping plover pairs there in 1999 appeared to have shifted to the Ninigret Conservation Area. Without consideration of these shifts in habitat use across a landscape, management for these species would be ineffective.

Some individuals preferred that the Service acquire and manage federal trust resources, and that the Refuge Complex continue to acquire these sites. Others emphasized partnerships to cooperatively protect and manage important habitats not currently on refuge land. Still others recommended a combination of Service acquisition and cooperative management to provide the greatest long-term benefit to resources. At public meetings and in our workbooks, many responses suggested specific areas needing protection, particularly wetlands threatened by development. Some individuals we spoke with especially supported our acquiring land occupied by endangered or threatened species.

The alternatives in the draft CCP/EA offered various levels of Service land acquisition, ranging from lands within the currently approved acquisition boundaries only, to a considerable expansion of each refuge's acquisition boundary. They also evaluated our increased involvement in cooperative land protection off-refuge. Addressing this issue will help achieve Goal 3: Establish a land protection program that fully supports accomplishment of species, habitat, and ecosystem goals.

7. Assurance of access to credible information about resources regarding the Refuge Complex to ensure management decisions are based on the best available science.

We need to determine and prioritize what information reasonably could be collected to facilitate decision-making using the best available science. In particular, many individuals expressed concern over the lack of information available to fully evaluate impacts to wildlife and habitats from excessive public use. Others questioned the effectiveness of management actions that have not been adequately monitored and evaluated. Several university researchers and other partners encouraged our staff to prioritize baseline inventory needs, establish monitoring protocols to better evaluate management actions, and identify information needed to determine each refuge's contribution to the ecosystem.

Implementing the Service's *Policy on Maintaining the Biological Integrity, Diversity, and Environmental Health of the National Wildlife Refuge System* will require us to ascertain the natural conditions for each refuge and identify the natural communities, species, and ecological processes that are rare, declining, or unique. Opportunities to cooperate in collecting this information could be developed once the priorities have been identified. The alternatives in the draft CCP/EA offered different levels of pursuing this information. Addressing this issue will help achieve all of our goals for the Refuge Complex.

8. Management of public use and access.

The Refuge Improvement Act and Service policy require our enhanced consideration of opportunities for six priority wildlife-dependent uses (see above). Some level of each occurs on the Refuge Complex. Only those uses that are compatible with a refuge's purpose may be allowed. According to Service policy, all refuges are closed to any use until they are formally opened through the compatibility determination process.

The act also directs refuges to terminate immediately or phase out as expeditiously as practicable, existing uses determined to be not compatible. Non-wildlife-dependent uses exist on all the refuges, and some have been occurring for years. Examples include jogging, sunbathing and swimming, bicycling, and dog walking.

Public meetings input and workbook responses make it clear that public use on refuges is extremely important to most people. More than 90 percent ranked environmental education and interpretation and wildlife observation and photography very high as desirable public uses. Rarely, however, was there consensus on other public uses or just how much of each type to allow. Public opinion spans the entire spectrum from those wanting to open up refuges to non-wildlife-dependent activities, to those who want to close refuges to all public use to maintain an undisturbed sanctuary for wildlife.

The alternatives in the draft CCP/EA compared different levels and combinations of wildlife-dependent public use. Addressing this issue will help achieve Goal 4: Provide opportunities for high quality, compatible, wildlife-dependent public use with particular emphasis on environmental education and interpretation.

9. Hunting.

Hunting surfaced late in the scoping process as a key issue, perhaps because, initially, few viewed it as a possibility on the Refuge Complex. This issue was raised by Service personnel, by RI DEM biologists, and by individuals both for and against expanding hunting opportunities on the Refuge Complex. Those in support primarily are interested in deer hunting on all refuges, waterfowl hunting on

Chafee Refuge and Ninigret Refuge, and pheasant hunting on Block Island. Advocates of hunting refer to its inclusion as one of the six priority public uses that "...shall receive priority consideration in refuge planning and management" (1997 RefugeImprovement Act).

None of Ninigret Refuge is currently open to hunting, but RI DEM has expressed its interest in any new opportunities for hunting because rapid residential development in Rhode Island is confining public hunting opportunities to fewer and fewer areas.

The Service views managed or administrative hunts in areas where there are overabundant deer populations as an effective tool for regulating them. Responses generally agree that the overabundance of deer is a concern in Rhode Island, reflected in increased numbers of vehicle-deer collisions, increased complaints about deer browsing on commercial and residential landscape plantings, visible impacts on native vegetation, and higher concern about contracting Lyme disease.

Those opposed to hunting cited concerns with public safety, disturbance and harm to other wildlife species, and the impact to visitors engaged in the other five priority public uses. The latter results from the likelihood that significant portions of the refuges, due to their small sizes and configurations, would be closed to other activities during hunting. Some expressed the opinion that the refuges should function as a sanctuary for all native species, and that hunting is incongruous with that function.

The alternatives in the draft CCP/EA explored varying levels of hunting opportunities, from no hunting at all, to opening four refuges during State-regulated seasons for deer, waterfowl, and pheasant. Addressing this issue will help achieve both Goal 2: Maintain and/or restore natural ecological communities to promote healthy, functioning ecosystems, and Goal 4: Provide opportunities for high quality, compatible, wildlife-dependent public use with particular emphasis on environmental education and interpretation.

10. Opportunities for environmental education.

Responses so frequently mentioned increasing environmental educational opportunities across the Refuge Complex that our planning team decided it warranted special recognition. More than 90 percent of the workbook responses ranked environmental education and interpretation as one of their top three interests. The alternatives in the draft CCP/EA compared different levels of environmental educational opportunities and the different levels of partnerships so integral to implementing them on each of the five refuges. Addressing this issue will help achieve Goal 4: Provide opportunities for high quality, compatible, wildlife-dependent public use with particular emphasis on environmental education and interpretation.

11. Provision of staffing, operations, and maintenance support sufficient to accomplish goals and objectives.

The Refuge Complex lacks adequate funding and personnel to provide the programs and services desired by the public and to effectively meet the goals for this CCP. The alternatives in the draft CCP/EA compared different funding and staffing levels based on their proposed management strategies for dealing with the issues.

Addressing this issue will help achieve Goal 5: Provide Refuge Complex staffing, operations, and maintenance support to effectively accomplish refuge goals and objectives.

12. Increasing the visibility of the Fish and Wildlife Service.

Our lack of visibility on refuges was brought up repeatedly at public meetings and in the workbooks. Many people felt strongly about the need for more refuge staff to be present during peak visitation to increase resource protection and improve visitor services. Other recommendations to increase visibility included more visitor contact stations, increasing wildlife interpretation and environmental educational opportunities, a better location for a headquarters office, developing a Refuge Complex visitor center, improving existing visitor facilities (e.g., kiosks, interpretive signs on trails, etc.), increasing support for a volunteer program, and increasing community involvement.

Some people expressed an interest in seeing refuge staff enforce public use policy more consistently. Others argued it was unnecessary for Service personnel to be armed while patrolling beaches. The alternatives in the draft CCP/EA compared different levels of promoting our visibility and providing these services. Addressing this issue will help achieve both Goal 2: Maintain and/or restore natural ecological communities to promote healthy, functioning ecosystems, and Goal 4: Provide opportunities for high quality, compatible, wildlife-dependent public use with particular emphasis on environmental education and interpretation.

13. Need for improved facilities.

The Refuge Complex lacks a facilities plan establishing current and future needs for staff operations and visitor services. Many of its current facilities are inadequate. Its headquarters does not have enough office space to accommodate even current staff, and the visitor services area is limited to one rack of literature in the reception area. The alternatives in the draft CCP/EA compared opportunities for new or improved facilities to accommodate staff work space, increase the visibility of the Service and the Refuge Complex, and improve visitor services, including environmental education and interpretation. Addressing this issue will help achieve Goal 5: Provide Refuge Complex staffing, operations, and maintenance support to effectively accomplish refuge goals and objectives.

Chapter 3

Piping plover
USFWS photo

Refuge and Resource Descriptions

- Geographic/Ecosystem Setting
- Socioeconomic Setting
- Refuge Complex Administration
- Refuge Resources
- Cultural Resources
- Public Uses

Geographic/Ecosystem Setting

Landscape Formation

The movement of glaciers across New England created the land forms seen in Rhode Island today. The last of those great ice sheets occurred during the Wisconsin glacial period. Approximately 15,000 - 20,000 years ago, the glacier was in a state of equilibrium, where the melting rate of ice equaled the glacial rate of movement (Bell 1985). As the climate warmed 12,000 - 15,000 years ago, the glacier began its retreat, depositing pronounced land forms along its outermost edge. The southern coast of Rhode Island, including Block Island, is the farthest point the Wisconsin glacier reached in its southeastern frontal movement. The retreating glacier deposited rocks pushed by the front of its ice sheet in piles called moraines. These terminal or end moraines formed sinuous ridges up to 200 feet high. Block Island is part of the terminal moraine that includes Nantucket and parts of Long Island.

A second prominent moraine lies inland, the low ridge referred to as the Charlestown or Watch Hill moraine, stretching east to west parallel to U.S. Route 1. Glacial action also created other features in today's landscape: recessional moraines, outwash plains, kettle hole ponds, glacial lake deposits, deltas, and submerged gravel shoals. Prominent headlands like Sachuest Point are composed of glacial till, a mixture of silt-sized grains to boulder-sized deposits by the melting glacier.

Melting ice sheets caused the sea to rise rapidly across Block Island and Rhode Island Sounds until it reached its present level approximately 4,000 years ago. Wave action parallel to the shore continued to erode glacial deposits, creating the barrier spits. As the spits formed, they almost entirely sealed off the low-lying areas between the headlands and the ocean, forming coastal lagoons connected to the sea by narrow inlets. These became the coastal salt ponds we see today. Through the 1700's, all of the coastal salt ponds had direct, seasonally open connections to the ocean (RI CRMC 1984). The effects of erosion through time have shifted the salt ponds and barrier spits gradually landward (RI CRMC 1998).

The bedrock formations of southern Rhode Island include the Blackstone series of metamorphic rock along its southern coastal border (including most of Westerly, Charlestown and South Kingstown), granite rock of various ages (including most of Narragansett and Middletown and parts of Westerly and Charlestown), and Pennsylvanian sedimentary rock in most of south central Rhode Island (including Richmond, much of South Kingstown, and most of Hopkinton). Most of the soils around the refuges are fine sandy loams or silt loams.

Historical Influences on Landscape Vegetation

The upland forests of southern Rhode Island are classified by Kuchler (1964) as oak-hickory forest; while most of northern Rhode Island is classified as oak-pitch pine forest. Historic land use practices promoted this forest type.

As early as 12,000 years ago, Native Americans began occupying the area. Documented evidence places the first intensive occupation of the salt pond region during the late Archaic period (5,000 to 3,000 years ago). Native American camps from more than 4,000 years ago are known to have existed at one location along the shore of Ninigret Pond. However, societies of that time were primarily hunter-gatherer with little agriculture; broad changes to landscape vegetation probably did not occur.

During the Woodland Period (3000 - 450 years ago), larger, semi-permanent or recurrently occupied camps became coastal settlements. Fortified villages are known to have existed in some locations. Maize horticulture became prominent, which likely resulted in small clearings. Larger clearings and burnings to control the movement of deer and upland birds may have occurred, and the first pronounced clearing of land along the coast for settlements, game management, and agriculture. Much of this land was cleared by cutting and burning, which favored resprouting by hardwood species like oak, hickory, and red maple.

The role fire may have played in shaping landscape vegetation is not well known. Evidence of fire has been observed in charcoal layers at Ninigret Refuge. Soil cores dug at most points on the refuge reveal charcoal below the historic farmers plow zone, approximately 10 inches soil depth. The dates attributed to these fires, coupled with their locations, suggest early Native Americans used fire extensively and purposefully.

Although small areas of land were cleared and more or less permanently settled by early Native Americans, it was European settlement and expansion in the 1600's that exponentially escalated the conversion of forests to agriculture. The eighteenth century Rhode Island plantation era "...required massive land clearing of the forests that had dominated the landscapes for the last 8,000 years" (USFWS 1999). During the mid-nineteenth century, an estimated 85 percent of southern New England was converted to field and pasture. Any woods remaining often were managed for firewood (Jorgensen 1977).

A detailed report on the archeological history of the Refuge Complex is available from the Refuge Complex office on request (Jacobson USFWS).

Contemporary Influences on the Landscape

The major natural disturbances affecting the coastline today are hurricanes and winter ice-storms. Hurricanes have the greatest impact, by far. The straight border of barrier beaches separated from the mainland by tidal wetlands and coastal salt ponds characterizes a coastline influenced by frequent storms. Wind and waves pick up loose sand and sediment and move it along the shoreline or back out to sea, allowing occasional overwash of barrier beaches and breaching of coastal ponds. Overwash, tidal currents, longshore currents, and rip currents are all mechanisms transporting sediment along the barrier beaches (RI CRMC 1998).

Fall and winter storms combining wind, rain, and waves are the predominant physical process shaping this landscape today. "Nor'easters" are well known along the New England coast in winter, winds generated offshore from the southeast, can actually be more destructive to the south shore, because of its exposure to the open ocean. The draft Salt Pond Region Special Area Management Plan describes the geologic, wave, and wind action for the South Shore, including details on how sediment movement constantly reshapes this dynamic landscape (RI CRMC 1998).

The Great New England Hurricane of 1938 was the most recent 100-year storm, one of immense power along the coast. Not only did winds reach speeds up to 240 miles per hour, but also a spring high tide created a storm surge between 10 and 15 feet. Storms of this magnitude are suspected to have occurred only four other times in recorded history: 1635, 1683, 1815, and 1821 (Bell 1985). Smaller hurricanes are less powerful but more frequent than the hurricane of 1938. Hurricanes in 1944, 1954, 1955, 1960, 1976, and Hurricane Bob in 1991 each left its mark on the coastline.

Human influences on sustaining the form and function of coastal landscapes and ecosystems over the long term are predominantly negative. Attempts to stabilize the beach system by constructing jetties or breach ways and planting beach grass have greatly affected the natural dynamics of this system by interrupting the natural flow of waves and sediment. In fact, the breach ways connecting the ponds to the ocean and one pond to another are the single greatest human impact on the ecology of coastal ponds (RI CRMC 1984).

Military installations directly impacted the landscapes that include Ninigret Refuge and Sachuest Point Refuge. From the 1940's through the 1960's, Ninigret Refuge was a U.S. Naval Auxiliary Landing Field. More than 70 acres of tree and shrub vegetation were cleared and maintained as asphalt runways and taxiways. Adjacent areas maintained as grasslands were planted with non-native species like larch and autumn olive. Between 1945 and 1973, 107 acres at the center of the Sachuest Point peninsula were used as an Army Coastal Defense site and a Navy firing range. Around a more recent Naval communications center, mowing and the use of herbicides maintained the vegetation in a low shrub-grasslands structure. A separate report on the history of the Sachuest Point Naval facility, entitled "Historical Perspectives on Establishing Sachuest Point Refuge" (Walker 1995), is available upon request at the refuge visitor center.

Introducing non-native, invasive plants, diverting or draining coastal wetlands for development, converting uplands for residential use, and spilling oil are other significant human impacts on the coastal landscape. Recent studies indicate that the greatest threats to Rhode Island's estuaries and coastal salt ponds are septic systems and road runoff (RI DEM 1996). More studies are needed to establish the extent to which each of these factors influences Refuge Complex ecosystems.

On Rhode Island's upland landscape, a combination of management and natural succession has allowed forests to make a comeback. The State Division of Forest Environment estimates that 300,000 acres of privately owned forest plus 45,000 acres of State-managed forest make up 45 percent of the State's land area. Their estimate places 80 percent of the privately owned forest in tracts from 1 to 10 acres in size, which are difficult to manage as forest and are rapidly being converted to residential areas (RI DEM 1996).

Ecosystem Delineations

The Service emphasizes an ecosystem approach to conservation, typically using large river watersheds to define ecosystems. Rhode Island falls within our Connecticut River/Long Island Sound Ecosystem (map 1-3).

Another commonly used delineation of ecosystems was developed by Bailey (USDA 1978, expanded 1995). These ecologically based map units often are used in landscape-level analyses. An ecoregion is first divided into a domain, then a division, a province, a section, and a subsection. Each level defines in greater detail its geomorphology, geology, soil, climate, potential vegetation, surface water, and current human use. Each of these resource attributes has implications for resource management. For example, opportunities to restore native grasslands may be limited by soil types, potential vegetation, and the extent of human impacts on the natural environment. Rhode Island falls within the Humid Temperate Domain, Hot Continental Division, Eastern Broadleaf Forest Province, and Lower New England Section.

Climate

Cold winters and warm summers with a moderating ocean influence characterize Rhode Island's climate. Winter temperatures average 30° F, with lowest temperatures ranging between -10° F and -20° F. Summer temperatures average 70° F, and peak in the 90s. Annual precipitation averages 44 to 48 inches, evenly distributed throughout the year. Thunderstorms occur throughout the summer (USFWS 1989).

Air Quality

The Clean Air Act establishes Class I, II, and III areas with limits on the amount of "criteria air pollutants" that can exist in pre-defined geographic areas. Examples of criteria air pollutants are smog (primarily ground-level ozone), particulate matter, and carbon monoxide. Class I areas allow very little additional deterioration of air quality (e.g. Wilderness Areas); Class II areas allow for more deterioration; and Class III areas allow even more. All of Rhode Island is currently classified as a Class II area. The U.S. Environmental Protection Agency (EPA) has designated the entire State a serious non-attainment area for ozone. That designation resulted in stricter automobile emissions standards designed to reduce emissions by 24 percent between 1990 and 1999.

Socio-economic Factors

The Refuge Complex lies close to some of the largest population centers on the east coast. The New York City metropolitan area, population 8.5 million, is 2.5 hours to the southeast. Metropolitan Boston, population 3.2 million, is 2 hours to the north. Hartford, with a population of 140,000, is 1.5 hours to the northwest, and Providence, population 161,000, is 45 minutes to the north (U.S. Census Bureau 1996 estimates and 1990 U.S. Census).

According to those estimates, the population of Rhode Island is about 1 million; 94 percent live in metropolitan areas (cf. the national average of 80 percent) and 6 percent in rural areas. South County, which includes Ninigret Refuge , Trustom Pond Refuge , and Chafee Refuge , has the fastest growing population and the highest number of building permits issued annually (RI CRMC 1998). South County population figures between 1990 and 1996 increased 7.4 percent, 4.6 percent, and 5.3 percent respectively in Charlestown, Narragansett, and South Kingstown, while Middletown's population decreased by 1.4 percent. The Town of New Shoreham, which includes Block Island, had a population increase of 10.8 percent. The population for the entire state of Rhode Island decreased by 1.3 percent over the same period (http://www.riedc.com).

The Refuge Complex directly contributes to the economies of Charlestown, South Kingstown, Narragansett, Middletown, and New Shoreham through refuge revenue sharing payments. The Federal Government does not pay property tax; it does pay refuge revenue sharing directly to cities and towns each year, based on the fair market value of refuge lands. The revenue sharing formula calculates three-quarters of 1 percent of the fair market value of refuge lands as the maximum amount payable each year. An appraisal updated every five years keeps their fair market value current. The actual amount of revenue sharing paid each year varies, depending on what portion of the maximum amount Congress appropriates that year (rarely the maximum). Figure 3-1 depicts refuge revenue sharing payments to those towns for the fiscal year 2000.

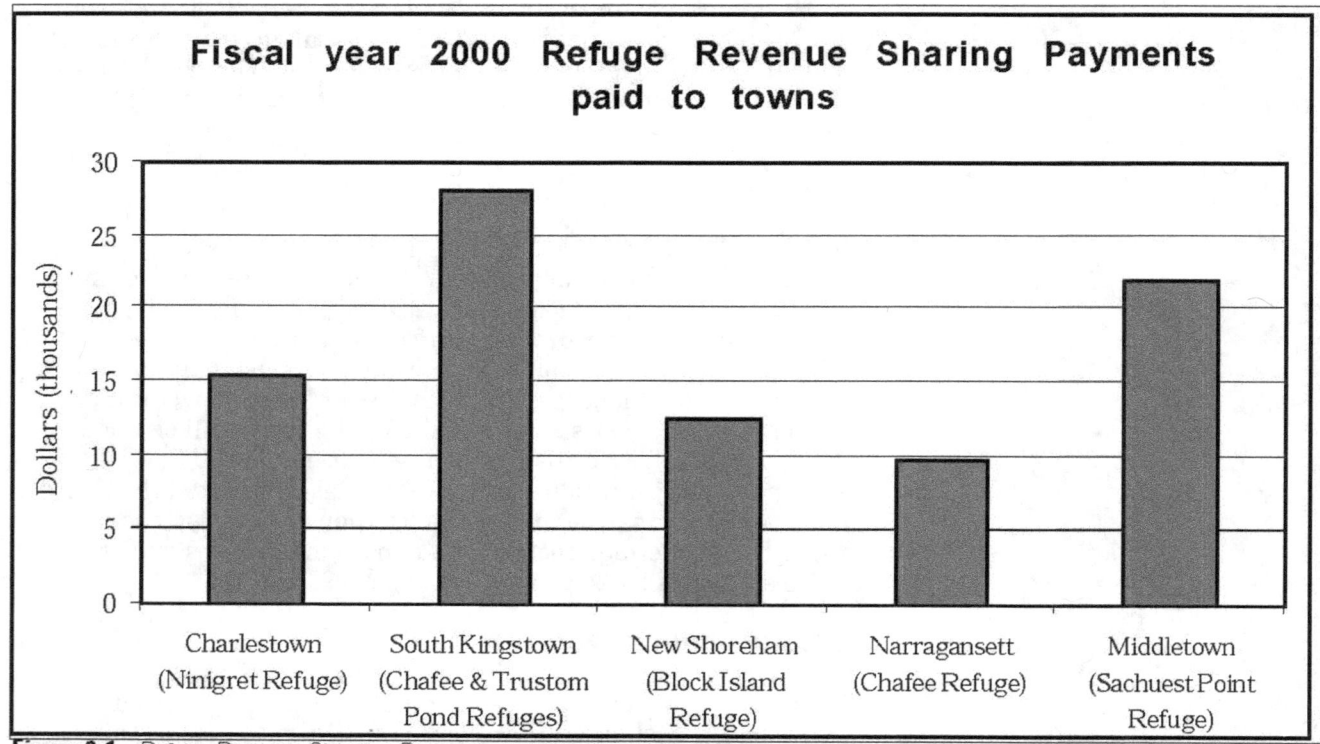

Figure 3-1. *Refuge Revenue Sharing Payments made to towns in 2000.*

The University of Rhode Island Department of Resource Economics (Spring 1997) reports that travel and tourism is the State's fastest growing industry. In 1996, it generated $1.7 billion. The number of visitors to the State in 1997 increased at a rate twice the national average. Also in 1997, Rhode Island's services industry, which includes those in health, business, and education, comprised the largest wage and salary employment at 34 percent (RI EDC 1997). Between 1987 and 1997, the services industry increased by 37 percent, while the manufacturing industry decreased by 37 percent.

In all the communities surrounding the refuges, travel and tourism and the services that support them contribute substantially to local economies. According to Ann O'Neill, President of the South County Tourism Council (O'Neill 1999), the tourist season lasts from April through October, with peak activity during the summer months. Responses to our workbooks confirm that beaches and water-associated recreation are the primary attractions for visitors with destinations along the Rhode Island coast.

Current travel and tourism literature does not feature the Refuge Complex. According to Ms. O'Neill, its refuges are not well known as tourist destinations, although many visitors discover them during their visit and enjoy the scenery and open space they provide. They are small enough to explore in one day, and generally do not prompt an additional night's lodging. Ms. O'Neill stated that, since the Tourism Council is trying to showcase a greater mix of outdoor recreational opportunities in South County, the Refuge Complex will figure more prominently in future promotional material.

The greatest contribution by the Refuge Complex to the local economy comes from the values attributed to the preservation of open space (NPS 1992). We represent those values using three indicators, below: Cost of Community Services; Property Values; and Public Willingness to Pay.

Cost of Community Services compares the cost per dollar of revenue generated by residential or commercial development to that of revenue generated by an open space designation. On the one hand, residential development expands the tax base, but the costs of increased infrastructure and public services (schools, utilities, emergency services, etc.) often offset any increase in revenue. On the other hand, undeveloped land requires few town services and places little pressure on the local infrastructure. The cost per dollar of revenue generated by commercial land typically falls between those of residential and open space.

The American Farmland Trust (1989, 1992, and 1993) and the Commonwealth Research Group (1995) evaluated community revenues and expenses associated with open space vs. residential and commercial development. All available information on the New England States shows that open space and commercial development produced more revenues than costs, while the opposite was true for residential land.

Conversations with local realtors and appraisers helped us evaluate the refuges' influence on property values. Two South County realtors and one realtor/appraiser confirmed that properties adjacent to refuges generally are valued higher (Gross, et al. 1998). That value is realized through increased sales price/acre in properties adjacent to a refuge, compared to otherwise similar properties, and by how quickly those properties sell. Properties with views protected by their proximity to a refuge exhibit an even greater difference. All the realtors estimated, but none with any certainty, that properties adjacent to refuges may realize from 1- to 4-percent increases in property value. All the realtors we spoke with use a property's adjacency to a refuge as an important advertising asset.

Public Willingness to Pay is a method for estimating the monetary value of ecosystem goods and services by determining how much the public would be willing to pay, either in taxes, fees, or opportunity costs, to preserve ecosystem values. In Rhode Island, where coastal ecosystems are threatened by development-at-large, we have used Willingness to Pay to estimate the value of open space preservation.

Rhode Islanders consistently and overwhelmingly vote for bond measures to protect open space. Local and State-wide bond measures passed in 1985, 1986, 1987, and 1989, invested more than $100 million in acquiring land for recreation and open space. A State-wide bond in 1998 passed an additional $15 million specifically for protecting open space (RI CRMC 1998).

Refuge Complex Administration

Staffing and Budget

Table 3-1. *Refuge Complex staffing levels and budgets between 1995 - 1999.*

Fiscal year	Operations	Maintenance	Full time staff	Seasonal staff
1995	$216,299	$85,700	7	3
1996	355,715	23,900	7	3
1997	350,700	97,700	8	4
1998	428,400	171,000	8	4
1999	441,900	28,000	9	2

Annual budget appropriations are highly variable, and commensurately affect our staffing levels. Table 3-1 summarizes budget and staffing levels from 1995 to 1999. Fluctuations reflect funding for special projects, moving costs for new employees, or large equipment purchases. Most of the funding is earmarked; very little discretionary funding is available.

Resource Protection and Visitor Safety

Law enforcement officers, with full authority to enforce federal regulations, are required to ensure resource protection and visitor safety. Three permanent refuge staff have been assigned collateral duties for law enforcement at any time during the course of refuge operations, but those collateral duties draw staff time and resources away from other important programs. We typically hire up to three seasonal staff with law enforcement authority each year.

During the past 5 years, formal notices of violation averaged 15 per year. They typically involved vehicle and pedestrian trespass, vandalism, and waterfowl hunting in closed areas. Well over 100 verbal warnings are also given each year, typically for inadvertently walking or driving in closed areas, littering, walking dogs in a closed area or off-leash, bicycling in closed areas, and digging plants. In 1993, a Trail Warden program began using volunteers to assist in documenting violations. Wardens also inform visitors of public use policy and permitted activities.

Refuge Complex Office

The Refuge Complex office currently lies in the Shoreline Plaza strip mall in Charlestown. In addition to housing our staff, it also houses our Division of Ecological Services Southern New England/New York Bight Coastal Ecosystem Program five-member staff, an Atlantic Coast Joint Venture staff person, and Friends of the National Wildlife Refuges of Rhode Island.

An environmental assessment was written in 2000, which determined a new location for a Refuge Headquarters and Visitor Center. The new building will be located on Deer Run Road (off Route 1) in Charlestown, RI. The building is currently being designed, with construction to begin in 2003.

Refuge Resources

Physical Resources

Geology and Hydrology

Most of Ninigret Refuge has a very high water table (6'-10' below the surface). Military excavations created several ponds as a result. Most of these man-made ponds are small and fairly unproductive, with steep sides and gravel bottoms. No natural streams exist on the refuge. The Navy constructed a series of ditches designed to direct runoff from the runways into Ninigret Pond. These ditches are responsible for reducing the salinity in at least two salt marshes, allowing an invasive plant species (*Phragmites spp.*) to take over these wetlands.

Some evidence suggests that the creation of runways and the resulting compaction of the underlying silt created a barrier impervious to water, causing runoff. After the recent removal of asphalt runway, some ponds are still forming, indicating this compacted silt layer still exists, and might need to be broken through to prevent frost-heaving of newly planted native grasses.

Topography and Soils

Most of the 701-acre refuge is located on a coastal outwash plain emanating from the base of the Charlestown Moraine. The refuge area is typical of coastal sandplain characterized by relatively flat terrain and sandy soils derived from sorted silt, sand, and gravel that flowed out from glacial meltwaters. Most soils on the Refuge are fine sand and silt loams in the Bridgehampton series and have very low levels of nutrients and organic matter. A high gravel content also characterizes refuge subsoil.

Biological Resources

Wetlands

Approximately 9% of Ninigret Refuge is wetland, including salt marsh, small, man-made ponds, forested and scrub-shrub wetlands, and emergent wetlands with varying amounts of open water. Most natural freshwater wetlands on the refuge are glacial kettle holes. The refuge contains at least 13 permanent ponds. Some tidal ponds on its mainland portion have restricted tidal flow due to siltation, and have become increasingly fresh. Most of the salt marsh acreage exists on the barrier beach parcel.

Unfortunately, most of the wetlands have diminished wildlife value because of the presence of Phragmites. Phragmites indicate a disturbed wetland, especially where the natural flushing of salt water has been altered, salinity has declined, or where sediment loading has occurred. The monotypic, virtually impenetrable stands of Phragmites choke out native plants, and provide little suitable food or cover for wildlife. Besides Phragmites, other dominant plants in the emergent freshwater wetlands are broad-leaved cattail (*Typha latifolia*), and a variety of sedges and rushes (*Juncus spp.*, *Eleocharis spp.*, *Scirpus spp.*). A portion of a red maple swamp lies on the western edge of the refuge. Several scrub-shrub wetlands are scattered throughout the area, dominated by buttonbush (*Cephalanthus occidentalis*), swamp rose (*Rosa palustris*), and swamp loosestrife (*Decodon verticillatus*).

Buried wetlands

Upon removal of the first segments of asphalt runway, evidence of several small wetlands, former vernal pools, were found buried under their gravel base. Aerial photographs in 1939 identified a total of five original wetland sites, which predate runway construction. At least two sites were located in 1997 by the presence of hydric soils and the remains of wetland seeds and plants. One of these wetlands had remnants of pinnate-leaved water milfoil (*Myriophyllum pinnatum*), a species that has not been reported in Rhode Island since 1913. Both sites have hydric soils about 40 inches below the surface and have scattered bulrush seeds and stems and other native wetland plant parts. Based on the 1939 aerial photographs, there appears to be at least one more site that remains buried underneath the runways.

The refuge biologist completed a management plan to restore the wetlands (1998) that includes mechanically removing layers of silt until the hydric soils are reached. The area to be disturbed is shaped roughly like a large footprint approximately 370 feet long and 110 feet at its widest point. Removed soils would be stockpiled on two adjacent sites and graded to create sloping mounds. The wetland edges would be seeded with native grasses. This project has not been funded.

Land use and dominant land cover types

(see table 3-2, following page)

Ninigret Pond: The open water of Ninigret Pond is not technically part of the refuge; however, the refuge does include approximately 3 miles of its shoreline, and another mile of shoreline along Foster's Cove. The presence of Ninigret Pond is a significant attraction to wildlife and refuge visitors and thus, has a direct influence on use and management of refuge land. For example, most refuge trails for viewing wildlife and scenery access the pond.

Ninigret Pond is the largest of the South Shore salt ponds, with an area of 1,711 acres and an average depth of 4 feet. It also has the largest associated watershed, 6,025 acres. The construction of a permanent breachway in 1962 to stabilize the pond radically changed its ecology, as evidenced by a depletion of the formerly productive estuarine fisheries. Habitat degradation includes the loss of 40 percent of its eelgrass beds over the last 32 years due to sedimentation and nutrient loading (RI CRMC 1998).

Water quality in Ninigret Pond is poor, as evidenced by elevated levels of nitrogen and fecal coliform bacteria (RI CRMC 1998). Symptoms of eutrophication from excessive nutrient loading include surface algal scum and discolored water. In 1996, the eastern portion of Ninigret Pond (where it connects to Green Hill Pond) was permanently closed to shell fishing due to the health risks associated with elevated fecal coliform bacteria.

Table 3-2. *Land use/dominant land cover types on Ninigret Refuge. (Based on aerial photo interpretation by J. Stone)*

Cover type	Acreage	Percent
Developed	64.5	9.2%
Native emergent wetland	9.8	1.4
Native forest upland	412.9	58.8
Native forest wetland	4.6	0.7
Native grass	40.6	5.8
Native shrub upland	88.4	12.6
Native shrub wetland	10.6	1.5
Non-native emergent wetland	32.2	4.6
Non-native shrub upland	16.3	2.3
Sand	9.6	1.4
Vegetated sand dunes	4.6	0.7
Water	7.6	1.0
Total	**701.7**	**100%**

Vegetation

Table 3-2 displays the dominant land cover types for Ninigret Refuge. A mosaic of diverse vegetation types covers the refuge, composed of approximately 91 percent upland and nineq percent wetland. More than 400 species of plants have been identified on the refuge, and recent plant surveys have rediscovered several species of plants which had not been recorded in Rhode Island for many years. A plant species list for Ninigret Refuge is available upon request from the refuge office (George 1999).

Grasslands

The Rhode Island Natural Heritage Program identifies coastal sandplain grasslands as a globally rare community (G2 & G3) under its ranking system. Only remnant patches of these native grasslands exist on Ninigret Refuge, and much of what remains is overgrown by shrubs and trees or dominated by forbs. The suitability of the refuge to many grassland-dependent species has declined or has been eliminated as a result of the succession to shrubs and trees. Approximately six percent of the refuge currently consists of herbaceous vegetation dominated by switchgrass (*Panicum virgatum*) and rough-leaved goldenrod (*Solidago rugosa*).

In July 1997, an environmental assessment was approved for habitat restoration at the refuge. Its stated goals are to restore native coastal sandplain grassland habitat and associated wildlife, especially those declining regionally, and to sustain the biological communities. The project would restore 60 acres of asphalt runway and 10 acres of stabilized gravel to native grasslands, and create an American with Disabilities Act (ADA) accessible trail system.

An additional 150 acres of grassland are currently maintained or will be created from shrubland through mowing and hydroaxing. Mowing and hydroaxing serve to keep woody vegetation from getting established in existing grasslands, or to set back succession in shrublands in an attempt to simulate the structure of grasslands.

We began the runway restoration project in 1997. Eighteen acres of runway were removed in a cooperative venture with the Army Reserve Unit during 1997 and 1998; refuge staff removed an additional 9 acres, and Navy Seabee Reserves removed an additional 15 acres in 1999. The original plan was to complete the asphalt removal in 2000.

To prepare for planting, rocks were windrowed and dumped into an excavated hole, or piled to the side. Approximately five acres were prepared in 1998 using a York rake on a farm tractor. The five acres were then fertilized and seeded with native grasses (predominantly little bluestem and switchgrass). So far, the restoration has been successful. Pennsylvanian sedge (*Carex pensylvanica*), sheep fescue (*Festuca filiformis*), switchgrass, blue-eyed grass (*Sisyrinchium atlanticum*), slender blue flag (*Iris prismatica*), and numerous goldenrods have established themselves in the restored sites. An additional 18 acres of native grasslands were planted in 1999. The area will be maintained through mechanical and chemical treatments.

Encroaching woody vegetation is continually a problem in the restored areas. Fifteen acres of red cedar and shrubs adjacent to the runways were hydroaxed in 1998. Another small field was prescription-burned in May 1998 to determine if this was a viable method for controlling woody vegetation in grasslands. Garlon 3A, an herbicide, was also tested on woody vegetation. The burned and herbicide areas are still being monitored to determine effectiveness. The Coastal Sandplain Grassland Restoration EA and the Ninigret Refuge Upland Management Plan (draft) describe additional strategies for restoring grassland habitat. A 1998 Progress Report on the restoration project makes several recommendations for maintaining restored areas (Flores 1998).

Restoring the grasslands may offer the opportunity to reintroduce plant species of concern, such as sandplain gerardia (federal-listed endangered), bushy rockrose (former federal candidate and endangered RI), and New England blazing star (former federal candidate and endangered RI).

A unique rare plant site, containing six species the State considers rare or endangered, lies within the grassland habitat on Ninigret Refuge. The rare species include colicroot (*Aletris farinosa*), slimspike three-awn (*Aristida longespica*), yellow-fringed orchids (*Platanthera ciliaris*), tall- and few-flowered nutrushes (*Scleria triglomerata, S. paucifolia*), and Indiangrass (*Sorgastrum nutans*). This unique assemblage resulted in a study recently published in Northeastern Naturalist (Killingbeck, et al. 1998). Extensive vegetation analysis and evaluation of site characteristics were done in 1996. Permanent vegetation monitoring transects were established as well (Killingbeck and Deegan 1996). Woody vegetation covered an average 56 percent of the quadrants sampled. Evidence from soil data indicates the site was previously disturbed because the topsoil and organic matter were non-existent in the core area. The site evaluation indicated a significant increase in the percent cover of Drosera, lichens, moss, and unvegetated soil within the core area, as opposed to adjacent sites without rare plants.

Shrublands

Approximately 16 percent of the refuge is upland shrub habitat. Shrubland communities vary in height and composition but are usually dominated by northern arrowwood (*Viburnum dentatum*), sumacs (*Rhus spp.*), bayberry (*Myrica pensylvanica*), highbush blueberry (*Vaccinium corymbosum*), or shadbush (*Amelanchier canadensis*). Most shrubs average 9' to 12' tall. Non-native plants such as Asian bittersweet dominate about 15 acres and have affected upland areas by crowding out native trees and shrubs.

Forests

The forest cover type has increased the most in the past 15 years, and now totals 413 acres, or 59 percent of the refuge. On forested refuge lands below Route 1, red maple and black cherry (*Prunus serotina*) dominate upland forest cover, followed by eastern red cedar (*Juniperus virginiana*), quaking aspen (*Populus tremuloides*), and gray birch (*Betula populifolia*). Red maple dominates the forested wetlands. Some remnant pitch pine (*Pinus rigida*) is also found on the refuge. The oldest forest stands occur on the western edge of Ninigret Refuge and within an isolated peninsula near the shrub wetland in the center of the refuge.

The two refuge tracts north of Route 1, totaling 292 acres, are upland deciduous forest dominated by various oaks, hickory, and red maple, followed by eastern red cedar and white pine.

Invasive Plants

Intensive surveys have shown invasive plants to be wide-spread on Ninigret Refuge at varying densities. Most of these are strong pioneer species that establish quickly and reproduce prolifically. Since they are so prolific, they will out-compete native vegetation and create a monoculture. While some of these species provide cover and food for wildlife, their dominance of the landscape will ultimately decrease biodiversity on the refuge.

Asian bittersweet and *Phragmites* are two of the most common invasive plants on the refuge, and dominate cover on 15 and 32 acres, respectively. The refuge is currently working with the University of Rhode Island on an experimental release of a European moth to control *Phragmites*. Autumn olive is also fairly common on the refuge, and was actually planted during the 1980's along the runways as wildlife food. This species occupies about 4 acres and continues its aggressive spread. Autumn olive will have to be controlled if the grasslands restoration project is to succeed.

Several species of honeysuckle are also found throughout refuge lands, comprising about 14 acres total. Honeysuckles exist at lower densities than the other invasive species, and are found in more shaded areas.

Threatened and Endangered Species

All threatened and endangered species and other species of concern for the Refuge Complex are listed in Appendix A, Trust Species and Other Species and Habitats of Management Concern.

Federal-listed: The bald eagle can be found at Ninigret Refuge during fall migration. Piping plover, a threatened species, have nested either on the barrier beach portion of the refuge or on the adjacent Ninigret Conservation Area every year since 1993. Piping plover typically breed on beaches from April through July, and into August if they re-nest after losing an early clutch. Symbolic fencing and nest exclosures are put in place each April. Fencing is taken down once chicks fledge. Figure 3-2 displays nesting success of piping plover on Rhode Island beaches.

State-listed: Appendix A also lists the status of State species of concern. Two State-listed grassland-dependent bird species, the grasshopper sparrow and the upland sandpiper, are focus species for grasslands management on Ninigret Refuge. The refuge was historical nesting habitat for both species (Enser 1999; Schneider and Pence 1992). Both species require large expanses of grassland for breeding and foraging. One study indicates grasshopper sparrows require 30 acres minimum breeding habitat (preferably 100 acres or greater) (Vickery, et al. 1994). Records for upland sandpiper suggest 150 acres are required (Schneider and Pence 1994). These species have different tolerances for interspersed patches of shrubland, the grasshopper sparrow being more tolerant. Their presence would validate the success of grasslands restoration.

South Shore Plover Program

Since 1992, refuge staff have helped monitor sites and protect piping plover on as many as nine other beaches along the South Coast. This highly successful cooperative management has resulted in a dramatic increase in the number of nesting plover and fledged chicks. The off-refuge plover protection program relies primarily on grants and cooperative funding with RI DEM. An annual report summarizes each year's statistics for nesting pairs and productivity and other relevant information on nesting sites, disturbance, and losses. It also recommends improvements in the program. These annual reports are available from the Refuge Complex office upon request.

Off-refuge management resembles the on-refuge program, with symbolic fencing of areas around the nest sites, exclosure fencing around each nest, monitoring nest activity, and educating the public on plovers and the problems associated with unleashed pets and litter. Since off-refuge management began in 1992, the number of nesting pairs has increased significantly at some sites. Figure 3-2 provides a summary of each site.

Figure 3-2. *Nesting success of piping plovers in coastal Rhode Island from 1992 to 1999.*

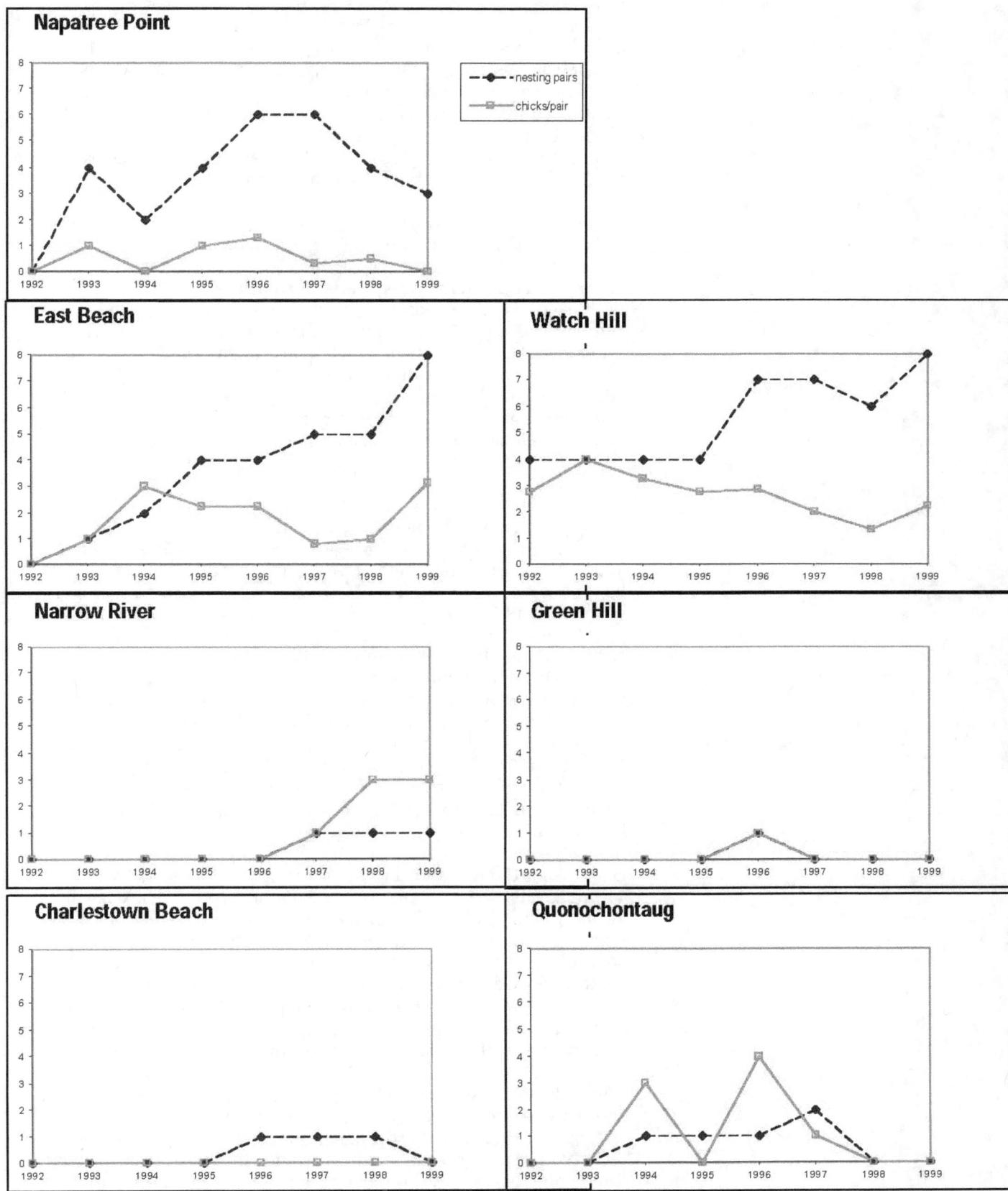

The field evaluation conducted by Hecht, et al. in 1999, determined that Ninigret Beach (referred to in Figure 3-2 as East Beach) has a provisional abundance objective of 20 pairs; Maschaug Beach (referred to in Figure 3-2 as Watch Hill) has a provisional abundance objective of nine pairs. The Revised Recovery Plan (1996) listed estimated carrying capacities of 10 pairs and 8 pairs for Ninigret and Maschaug Beaches, respectively. These figures should be interpreted as maximum carrying capacities, based on physical attributes only. Hecht noted the carrying capacity is subject to rapid change due to storms, changes in sand deposition and erosion patterns, and other beach-forming processes.

Least tern (*Sterna antillarium*), a State-listed species (threatened), has also benefitted from and responded favorably to strategies to protect nesting piping plover. At Moonstone Beach, exclosures around an entire tern colony and solar-powered electric fencing has been used to deter predators. Tern numbers on the beach have been increasing; RI DEM counted 160 individuals in 1998. Despite predator trapping, however, small mammalian predators like mink and red fox continue to significantly affect tern fledgling rates and adult survival. The fencing appears to be effective only against dogs; small mammals are able to get through. Terns do not always nest in the fenced area, further complicating their protection.

Birds

The wide variety of habitats have contributed to the great diversity of birds found on Ninigret Refuge. Approximately 70 species are known to nest on the refuge. Recent mist-netting on refuge lands has shown that gray catbirds (*Dumetella carolinensis*), common yellowthroats (*Geothlypis trichas*), and red- winged blackbirds (*Agelaius phoeniceus*) are the most abundant nesting birds in the shrub community (Eddleman 1993, 1994; Wallace 1995; Paton 1996, 1997, 1998). Breeding Bird Survey data indicates that the refuge may have one of the highest densities of nesting yellow-breasted chat in Rhode Island (Enser1998). Other birds using early successional shrub and grassland vegetation for nesting include white-eyed vireo, black-billed cuckoo, willow flycatcher, northern bobwhite, prairie warbler, and American woodcock. Recently, bobolink, eastern meadowlark, eastern bluebirds, and wild turkey have been found nesting on the refuge.

Birds using the wetlands include green herons, wood ducks, Virginia rails, swamp sparrows, and marsh wrens. The coastal location of the Refuge Complex provides vital stopover habitat for migratory birds seeking to quickly and safely accumulate energy stores. According to Moore, coastal scrub/shrub and dune/scrub habitats provide very high species richness and abundance (Moore, et al. 1995). Birds are primarily foraging on berries and insects. As residential development along the coast continues, maintaining and enhancing these habitats will become even more important.

Winter birds present on the refuge include northern harrier, short-eared owl, eastern bluebird, and a variety of sparrows. Waterfowl include black duck, mallard, American wigeon, and green-winged teal. Ninigret Pond is an important wintering area for bufflehead, common goldeneye, greater scaup, and red-breasted merganser. Table 3-3 summarizes waterfowl numbers at Ninigret Pond from 1992 to 1999.

Table 3-3. *Peak waterfowl numbers on Ninigret Pond from 1992 to 1999.*

	1992	1993	1994	1995	1996	1997	1998	1999
Mute swan	32	34	7	22	12	20	26	29
Snow goose	-	5	-	-	1	1	-	0
Brant	12	1	-	9	-	15	-	5
Canada goose	72	61	14	12	150	95	133	145
Wood duck	-	2	-	5	2	-	-	0
Green-winged teal	4	2	2	3	-	-	-	-
Blue winged teal	3	5	-	-	-	-	-	-
American black duck	102	497	346	224	155	237	188	168
Mallard	5	10	4	8	40	8	34	36
Gadwall	1	22	-	5	-	8	-	-
American wigeon	-	2	-	-	2	-	-	-
Canvasback		1	20	5	27	-	-	-
Redhead	-	2	2	-	-	-	-	-
Ring-necked duck	-	520	-	-	-	-	-	-
Greater scaup	37		346	200	400	350	534	172
Lesser scaup	-	-	1	-	15	225	306	4
Common eider	-	-	-	-	1	1	-	-
King eider	-	-	-	-	-	-	1	-
Oldsquaw	1	-	-	-	3	3	1	1
Black scoter	-	-	-	-	3	-	-	-
Surf scoter	1	-	1	5	3	-	-	1
White-winged scoter	8	24	-	3	-	-	-	-
Common goldeneye	2	750	401	252	310	159	81	225
Bufflehead	401	699	1725	700	949	924	864	815
Hooded merganser	2	2	1	4	9	26	34	16
Red breasted merganser	:	250	211	365	415	370	325	413
Ruddy duck	-	-	2	15	-	-	-	12
Northern pintail	-	-	-	-	-	-	-	1
Common merganser	-	22	290	-	14	9	15	11

Recent surveys for wintering greater scaup reveal that many of the waterfowl that feed in Ninigret Pond will rest at Trustom Pond during the day (Cohen 1998).

Mammals

Twenty-two species of mammals have been observed on the refuge. Large mammals include white-tailed deer (*Odocoileus virginianus*), coyote (*Canus latrans*), red squirrel (*Tamiasciurus hudsonicus*), red fox (*Vulpes fulva*), raccoon (*Procyon lotor*), striped skunk (*Mephites mephites*), and eastern cottontail (*Sylvilagus floridanus*). Mink (*Mustella vison*) and river otter (*Lutra canadensis*) have been observed on or adjacent to the refuge. Small mammals include eastern meadow vole (*Microtus pennsylvanicus*), white-footed mouse (*Peromyscus leucopus*) and woodland jumping mice (*Napaeozapus insignis*).

We suspect from the evidence of high browse line along trails and habitat edges that the white-tailed deer population is near or above carrying capacity at Ninigret Refuge. Deer are a potential threat to managing the rare native plant site. Although we have not begun studies to substantiate this concern, the sheer numbers and distribution of deer make it an eventuality. Permanent monitoring points at the rare plant site will allow further investigation of this issue.

Invertebrates

Surveys for deer ticks are the only invertebrate studies conducted on the refuge. Deer tick surveys indicate that Ninigret Refuge is a hotspot for ticks carrying Lyme disease, erlichiosis, and babesiosis. The refuge intends to coordinate with The Nature Conservancy's 5-year atlas project begun in 1998 to document dragonflies and damselflies throughout the State.

Amphibians and Reptiles

A report entitled "Amphibian Community Structure at the Rhode Island National Wildlife Refuge Complex" (Paton, et al. February 1999) focused primarily on Trustom Pond Refuge, but offers information on amphibians using Ninigret Refuge as well. The red maple swamp and the small pools scattered throughout the refuge likely provide the best habitats for amphibians. Amphibians generally do not occur within tidal waters because salt water dries their skin. Gray tree frogs (*Hyla versicolor*), spring peepers (*Pseudacris crucifer*) and green frogs (*Rana clamitans*) are the most abundant frog species. Red-backed salamanders (*Plethodon cinereus*) were the only members of that group found on the refuge, but other salamander species probably occur in the area. The report states that the amphibian communities at both Trustom Pond Refuge and Ninigret Refuge are relatively rich and thriving, and states the refuges are vital and critical to the conservation of amphibians in Rhode Island. Snapping, painted, and spotted turtles (*C. guttata*) are abundant in most of the ponds on the refuge. They are also known to occur in brackish water and may venture out into estuaries. Recently, eastern box turtles (*Terrepene carolina*) have been found in the uplands. Six species of snakes have also been observed on the refuge: eastern garter snake, ribbon snake (*T. sauritus*), northern water snake (*Natrix sipedon*), black racer (*Coluber constrictor*), eastern milk snake (*Lampropeltis triangulum*), and northern brown snake (*Storeria dekayi*).

Fish

Since Ninigret Pond is not technically part of the refuge, we do not manage the fisheries resource. According to the Coastal Salt Pond Special Area Management Plan, more than 100 species of finfish and shellfish utilize coastal salt ponds at some stage of their life cycle. The fisheries in Ninigret Pond are diverse, although quantitative information is scarce. It is widely perceived today that stocks of the most popular species such as quahogs, scallops, oysters, and flounder are all declining (RI CRMC 1998).

Cultural Resources

Past military activities have also affected archeological resources at Ninigret Refuge. Only a few areas have intact soils. Construction of the Charlestown Naval Auxiliary Landing Facility required massive earth moving, which would have impacted the integrity of many archeological sites. One is listed on the National Register of Historic Places for its historic use as a shellfish gathering site by the Narragansett Indians. Another, a burial site for the Narragansett Indians, was discovered during the runway construction and was recorded with the Rhode Island Historic Preservation and Heritage Commission (RI HPHC). The intact areas are considered highly sensitive for archeological resources. Studies of these sites have been limited in area and scope. No comprehensive archeological surveys have been done on the refuge.

Public Use

Until 1997, the three asphalt runways and two taxiways from the former naval air station composed approximately 5 miles of an 8-mile trail system on the refuge. All three runways provided visitors access to the shoreline of Ninigret Pond. The grasslands restoration project began removing the old runway in 1997, except for an 8'-wide swath that forms the base of the new trail system, which will be 3.8 miles in length. In addition to runways, the trail comprises old roads from the former Champlin Farm and from the naval base.

We also plan interpretive displays and kiosks to share information on landscape formation by glaciers, Native American use, naval aviation history, and colonial farming. Once completed, this "Trail Through Time" will involve a partnership among the Narragansett Indian Tribe, the Charlestown Airfield Memorial Committee, and the Frosty Drew Memorial Fund. One viewing platform overlooks Ninigret Pond at Grassy Point. A second viewing platform planned for the Foster Cove area has not been funded. Two kiosks stand along the east and west entrance and parking areas.

We completed improvements to the refuge entrance road in 2002, using Transportation Equity Act funds. Improved signs directing visitors to Ninigret Refuge are needed on U.S. Route 1. Current signs do not meet Refuge System standards, and visitors have commented that the existing highway sign, which reads "Ninigret Park Wildlife Refuge", causes confusion with the adjacent, town-managed Ninigret Park.

Special Management Areas

Contaminants

Department of Defense activities left four potential contaminant sites at the refuge. EPA lists them collectively as CERCLIS No. RI9143530260. Three of the four sites (Eastern Area Landfill, Burnpit Area, and Ninigret Wildlife Refuge Landfill) are located entirely on the refuge, while the On-site Landfill is located partly on Ninigret Park (Town of Charlestown). The U.S. Army Corps of Engineers (ACOE) has coordinated contaminant sampling and analysis at the sites since 1986. Various ACOE contractors have completed several different sampling and analysis studies. Each study has documented varying levels of contamination. The Burnpit Area, which served as a firefighter training site while the airfield was active appears to be the least contaminated.

The three landfills resulted from closure and demolition of the airfield prior to transfer of the property to the Service. Known contaminants include volatile organic compounds, semi-volatile organic compounds, pesticides, and metals. ACOE is continuing to assess the need to conduct additional sampling and environmental assessments, and is addressing EPA and RI DEM concerns, which may eventually lead to site remediation where necessary.

Military Debris

In addition to the CERCLIS sites, a tremendous amount of miscellaneous military debris exists on Ninigret Refuge, including the concrete light fixtures along the runways, the concrete hard stand (machine gun backstop), small buildings like the cinder block pump house and hydrant and several old bunkers, the explosives magazine, a number of telephone poles, an old gate, and concrete-reinforcing mesh.

Of particular interest is a simulated wooden aircraft carrier deck, complete with steel catapult rail. Shrubs have overgrown the deck, except for one portion intersected by a trail, and many of its timbers are rotting in the ground, but the catapult is still visible. Aviation interest groups have proposed it as a feature worthy of interpretation. The Aviation Historical Society (RI) has suggested that this simulated deck may be the only one of its type remaining. We may include it as a stop on an interpretive trail.

Military construction moved a lot of earth on Ninigret Refuge, leaving scattered piles of dirt and boulders. One of the runways was extended by backfilling between Hunter's Island and the mainland. Much of that fill was never capped, and is exposed in many areas.

Chapter 4

Redstart
USFWS photo

Management Direction

- Refuge Complex Vision
- Refuge Complex Goals
- General Refuge Management

Refuge Complex Vision

We developed this vision statement to provide a guiding philosophy and sense of purpose for the five refuge CCPs. It qualitatively describes the desired future character of the Refuge Complex through 2015 and beyond. We wrote in the present tense to provide a more motivating, positive, and compelling statement of purpose. It has guided, and will continue to guide, program emphases and priorities for each refuge in Rhode Island.

Freshwater wetland. *USFWS photo.*

`The Rhode Island National Wildlife Refuge Complex protects a unique collection of thriving coastal sandplain, coastal maritime, and beach strand communities, and represents some of the last undeveloped seacoast in southern New England. Leading the way in the protection and restoration of coastal wetlands, shrubland, and grassland habitats, the Refuge Complex contributes to the long-term conservation of migratory and resident native wildlife populations, and the recovery of endangered and threatened species. These refuges offer research opportunities and provide an outstanding showcase of habitat management for other landowners."

`The Refuge Complex is the premiere destination for visitors to coastal Rhode Island to engage in high quality, wildlife-dependent recreation. Hundreds of thousands of visitors are rewarded each year with inspiring vistas and exceptional opportunities to view wildlife in native habitats. Innovative environmental educational and interpretive programs motivate visitors to engage in better stewardship of coastal resources."

`Through partnerships and extensive outreach efforts, Refuge Complex staff are committed to accomplishing refuge goals and significantly contributing to the Mission of the National Wildlife Refuge System. This commitment will strengthen with the future, revitalizing the southern New England ecosystem for generations to come."

Refuge Complex Goals

Our planning team developed the following goals for the Refuge Complex after reviewing applicable laws and policies, regional plans, the Refuge Complex vision statement, the purpose of each refuge, and public comments. All the goals fully comply with Service policy and national and regional mandates.

Our Refuge Complex goals are intentionally broad, descriptive statements of purpose. They highlight specific elements of our vision statement and provide the foundation for our management emphasis. We identified Goal 1 as the top priority for the Refuge Complex; Goals 2-5 are not presented in any particular order.

Each goal is further refined by a series of objective statements. Objectives are incremental steps to be taken toward achieving a goal and define the management emphasis in measurable terms, where possible. Some of our objectives relate directly to habitat management, while others strive to meet population targets tied to species' recovery plans, or state or regional species plans. The strategies for each objective are specific actions, tools, techniques, considerations, or a combination of these, which may be used to achieve the objective. Objectives will be used directly in respective step-down plans, while strategies may be revised or modified to achieve the desired outcome.

Together, the goals and objectives are unifying elements of successful refuge management. They identify and focus management priorities, provide a context for resolving issues, and offer a critical link between refuge purpose(s), and the National Wildlife Refuge System Mission.

Integral to all the objectives under Goal 1 and Goal 2 is development in 2003 of a Habitat Management Plan (HMP) for the Refuge Complex. This will be the highest priority step-down plan to accomplish. We will write the plan using current resource information, but will update it based on new information, as needed. The purpose of the HMP will be to prevent the loss or degradation of habitat types, species assemblages, or natural processes significant to the Refuge Complex. It will identify habitat management actions that, to the extent practicable, restore and sustain viable populations of our focus species. The objectives and strategies identified below will all be incorporated into the HMP.

Once the HMP is developed, the Refuge Complex will develop a Species and Habitat Inventory and Monitoring Plan in 2004. Critical elements of the biological program to be inventoried or monitored will be identified, prioritized, and scheduled. This plan will also describe inventory and monitoring procedures, determine where data will be stored, and identify the interim and final reports to include. It will provide a critical connection between the HMP and credible, adaptive refuge management.

In addition, the Region is currently developing a Regional National Wildlife Refuge System Strategic Resources Plan (SRP). This plan will establish Regional goals and objectives for species and habitats based on landscape-scale analyses. Each refuge staff will then determine their respective refuge's contribution to implementing these objectives. As such, once the SRP is completed, the objectives and strategies outlined below may be modified.

The following goals, objectives, and strategies provide management direction for the refuge over the next 15 years. Unless otherwise noted, all work will be accomplished by the Service, primarily by Refuge Complex staff.

Goal 1: Protect and enhance federal trust resources and other species and habitats of special concern.

Objective 1.1
Meet or exceed a 5-year average of 1.5 fledged chicks/pair per year (1996 Revised Piping Plover Recovery Plan) on the Ninigret Refuge barrier beach nesting site. An additional annual objective is to meet or exceed the site's estimated nesting carrying capacity (estimated at 20 pairs in 1999 for the Ninigret Refuge-Ninigret Conservation Area site), which may vary from year to year given the dynamics of the beach ecosystem.

Background:

The 1996 Revised Recovery Plan for the Atlantic Coast Population of the Piping Plover (Federal-listed as threatened) describes the species status, habitat requirements, and limiting factors. The major factors contributing to the species' decline is the loss and degradation of habitat due to development and shoreline stabilization. The recovery objective is to remove the species from the List of Endangered and Threatened Wildlife and Plants by: 1) achieving well-distributed increases in numbers and productivity of breeding pairs, and 2) providing for long-term protection of breeding and wintering plovers and their habitat.

Objective 1.1 directly supports Recovery Criteria #1 and #3, which relate to maintaining a wide distribution of breeding pairs, and a consistent productivity and fledging rate. In general, we hope to achieve this by increasing the amount and duration of protection and monitoring of nesting sites, and through habitat improvements, as outlined below.

The Partners In Flight Bird Conservation Plan for Southern New England (Physiographic Area #9; draft Oct 2000) (PIF Plan) also lists several implementation strategies and management guidelines to achieve habitat objectives for piping plover, including monitoring and research, actively deterring predators, preventing human disturbances at nesting sites, and public education. All of these are incorporated as strategies in objectives 1.1 through 1.4 below.

The Ninigret Refuge piping plover nesting area extends beyond the refuge and includes the adjacent state-administered Ninigret Conservation Area. The nesting area has been monitored and managed in cooperation with both the Fish and Wildlife and State Parks Divisions of RI DEM. Near suitable nesting habitat, but on the back side of the dunes, is a small state campground. Refuge staff have been concerned that the presence of campers during the nesting season could pose a risk to nesting piping plover in the area. Trash is often implicated in attracting predators to a nesting area. In addition, campers in the area often bring dogs; at other nesting sites, unleashed dogs have been observed chasing adult plover off nest. However, in order to avoid the risk, we are proposing to work with RI DEM to move the campground away from suitable habitat.

Strategies:

■ Each year, continue to monitor for piping plover activities in suitable habitat areas at the Ninigret site beginning in early April. Install symbolic fencing around potential territories (above mean high tide line) to exclude public access when courtship behavior is observed. Fencing will remain in place until the birds have fledged (typically by August 15). Monitoring and management actions will meet or exceed the Service's 1994 *Guidelines for Managing Recreational Activities in Piping Plover Breeding Habitat on the U.S. Atlantic Coast To Avoid Take Under Section 9 of the Endangered Species Act* (Appendix G in the 1996 Recovery Plan).

■ Each year, continue to coordinate with the Service's Ecological Services Division and RI DEM prior to the nesting season.

- Continue to support RI DEM's seasonal (April 1 - Sept 15) vehicle closure on Ninigret Conservation Area's beach.

- In 2003, work with RI DEM to evaluate moving the State campground away from suitable piping plover nesting habitat, concentrating human activities in less sensitive areas, and thereby reducing direct and indirect human impacts in nesting areas.

- In 2003, reassess nesting carrying capacity on Ninigret Refuge barrier beach and adjacent Ninigret Conservation Area, last evaluated in 1999; repeat assessments on a three year basis.

Piping plover chick. *USFWS photo.*

Objective 1.2

Meet or exceed a 5-year average of 1.5 fledged chicks/pair per year (1996 Revised Piping Plover Recovery Plan) on at least six of the cooperatively managed piping plover nesting sites along Rhode Island's South Shore. An additional annual objective is to meet or exceed each site's estimated nesting carrying capacity, which may vary from year to year given the dynamics of the beach ecosystem.

Background:

In addition to the Trustom Pond, Block Island, and Ninigret refuge nesting areas, nine other active or potential piping plover nesting sites occur on Rhode Island's South Shore, off refuge lands, and are monitored as a cooperative venture between the refuge and the landowner. Besides the refuges, six sites have had consistent nesting attempts over the last 5 years. Our primary objective has been to protect all active piping plover nesting sites from direct impacts and to increase productivity and fledging rates to meet the recovery goal of a five year average of 1.5 fledged chicks/pair (This objective is also included in the Trustom Pond CCP because the South Shore cooperative management program is integrated between the refuges).

Strategies:

- Each year, continue to monitor piping plover activities in suitable habitat areas beginning in early April. Install symbolic fencing around potential nesting sites to exclude public access when courtship behavior is observed. Fencing will remain in place until birds have fledged (typically by August 15). Monitoring and management actions will meet or exceed the Service's 1994 *Guidelines for Managing Recreational Activities in Piping Plover Breeding Habitat on the U.S. Atlantic Coast To Avoid Take Under Section 9 of the Endangered Species Act* (Appendix G in the 1996 Recovery Plan).

- Prior to each nesting season, continue to coordinate with, and seek support from, the Service's Ecological Services Program, RI DEM, and respective landowners.

- In 2004, develop written cooperative agreements with at least five South Shore landowners with existing plover nesting sites, in order to formalize access permissions and to promote consistent management of piping plover nest sites.

- By 2004, hire a Rhode Island Piping Plover Coordinator* who will provide visibility and oversight to the South Shore and Refuge Complex piping plover programs, and facilitate interagency funding and cooperative management of the South Shore nesting areas.

- By 2007, coordinate with private landowners and towns to develop contingency plans in anticipation of unexpected events such as oil spills at nesting sites or the "pioneering" of new nest sites on recreational beaches.

*The Rhode Island Piping Plover Coordinator will a) coordinate outreach and education; b) complete cooperative agreements with private landowners (see above); c) coordinate with towns to develop contingency plans (see below); d)coordinate piping plover research on the refuges; e) hire seasonal biological technicians; f) seek outside funding to help support the South Shore program; g) coordinate habitat evaluations and monitoring (e.g. determine nesting carrying capacities, habitat parameters to monitor, and predator trapping effectiveness).

Objective 1.3
Each year, minimize predation of piping plover at nesting sites in support of nest productivity and fledging objectives.

Background:
According to the 1996 Recovery Plan and experience at Rhode Island nesting sites, predation is a major factor limiting piping plover reproductive success. Predation is highly site-specific, but evidence indicates that human activities are exacerbating natural predation levels by influencing the types, numbers, and activity patterns of predators. As a result, we are managing human activities as described in Objectives 1.1 and 1.2, and also trying to influence predator behavior at nesting sites. Our predator management includes the use of non-lethal strategies (e.g. visual deterrents, scare tactics, fenced exclosures), as well as the removal of animals.

Strategies:

- Continue to document statistics (productivity, fledging rates, nest losses, predation, etc.) in annual piping plover reports, and share information with Recovery Team Coordinator.

- Continue to minimize direct predation of piping plover at each nesting site through the use of exclosures and other non-lethal deterrents, and remove animals where it is warranted and feasible. Utilize recommended techniques in "Best Management Practices for Trapping Furbearers," a technical report to be completed by the Fur Resources Committee of the International Association of Fish and Wildlife Agencies, when available.

- By 2005, evaluate predation statistics to determine the effectiveness of predator management efforts at nesting sites. Adapt management accordingly.

Objectives 1.4
Within three years of CCP completion, fully develop a piping plover outreach and education program specifically targeting people using Rhode Island beaches.

Strategies:

- Continue to maintain the interpretive display on the Ninigret nesting site, including a mock nest exclosure display explaining its design and purpose, and install informational signs restricting public use.

- Continue annual coordination with the Friends Group to provide oversight, conduct public outreach and education, and help secure non-Service funding for the South Shore Piping Plover Program.

- Complete development of a barrier beach education kit for teachers.

- In 2003, develop an education and outreach plan for the piping plover program, which will include:

  - Identification of target audiences (e.g. beach front landowners, elected officials, tourists, and local school children);

  - Distribution of literature with RI DEM beach use permits, at beach entrance stations, and other focal points; and

  - A major exhibit at the new Visitor Center; and

  - An educational program integrated with local school curriculums.

- Work with the Friends Group and other partners to develop and implement the plan and secure funding for its initiatives.

- By 2004, hire at least two additional seasonal park aids to conduct outreach and education on-site or in the communities directly affected by piping plover management.

Objective 1.5
Determine the site-specific factors affecting Rhode Island piping plover nesting success and undertake actions recommended or accepted by the piping plover scientific community.

Strategies:

- Each year, the refuge biologist will coordinate with the Plover Recovery Team and other scientists to obtain new research results and share the effectiveness of management techniques.

- By 2004, work with partners to identify piping plover research needs for the Refuge Complex, with highest priority given to determining those factors most influencing chick survival on the refuges.

- By 2005, obtain funding to initiate the highest priority project.

Objective 1.6
Within two years of CCP completion, establish specific habitat management objectives for those birds considered to be a high conservation priority in the Partners In Flight (PIF) Area 9 Plan, Southern New England, and for which the refuge could make an important contribution to their conservation.

Background:
PIF Bird Conservation Plans are written for physiographic provinces with an overall goal to ensure the long term maintenance of healthy populations of landbirds. Rhode Island Refuges lie within PIF Physiographic Area 9, Southern New England. These plans identify species and habitats most in need of conservation, describe desired habitat conditions for these species, develop biological objectives, and recommend conservation actions.

The PIF Plan for Area 9 is not yet final, however, this CCP incorporates habitat objectives for certain landbird species identified in the draft PIF Plan (October 2000). These include piping plover (objectives 1.1 to 1.5), shrub- and grassland-dependent coastal Neotropical migrants, and maritime marshland species. Using information from the surveys identified below and the completed PIF Plan, we will be able to refine our land bird management objectives in the near future.

Strategies:

■ Continue annual bird monitoring associated with the 220 acre shrubland/grassland restoration on the refuge; conduct bi-weekly surveys during May and June of each year.

■ Continue coordination with the University of RI to conduct the Monitoring Avian Productivity and Survivorship (MAPS) project.

■ Continue to conduct refuge-wide Breeding Bird Surveys on a 3- to 5- year interval, biweekly during the breeding season, according to established protocol.

■ In 2003, utilize the "Partners in Flight Landbird Conservation Plan for Southern New England (Area 9)" (draft Oct 2000), and the Service's Region 5 Regional Resources Assessment to identify and prioritize those landbirds of highest management concern on the refuge, and assess how current management practices are impacting them. Determine which of these landbirds should be a focus for future management on the refuge, and write landbird objectives for the HMP.

■ In conjunction with development of the HMP, update refuge cover-type maps, adhering to National Vegetation Classification Standards.

Objective 1.7
Protect and sustain all marsh, wading and water bird breeding habitat on the refuge, especially maritime high marsh habitat capable of supporting salt marsh sharp-tailed sparrow.

Background:
According to the PIF Area 9 Plan, maritime marsh habitat is the habitat most in need of immediate conservation attention in this physiographic area due to the large number of priority species and the tremendous pressure from human development along the coastline. Substantial threats also exist in the form of human disturbance, pollution, increasing predator populations, and invasive, exotic species. Reducing these threats is the highest conservation concern to be addressed. Restoration of high salt marsh is also a priority.

Strategies:

■ By 2003, conduct saltmarsh sharp-tailed sparrow surveys in suitable habitat according to Regional protocol.

■ By 2005, initiate an inventory for marsh and wading birds, according to Regional protocol, at all high probability sites on the refuge to determine seasonal occupancy and nesting status. If occupied habitat is located, develop site plan.

■ Use the North American Waterbird Conservation Plan (once completed) to update management and monitoring strategies for species of conservation priority.

Objective 1.8
Protect and improve habitat quality for shorebirds at feeding and staging areas on the refuge.

Background:
Shorebirds annually migrate hundreds or thousands of miles between breeding and wintering grounds, often in one or a few long-distance non-stop flights. As such, migration staging areas, where birds rest and accumulate fat reserves before and during flight, are vitally important to many shorebird populations. Along the east coast, beaches are key locations. Long-term declines of shorebird numbers at migration staging areas along the Massachusetts coast have been attributed to conflicts between shorebirds and heavy human recreational use. Monitoring shorebirds during migration has not occurred consistently on Ninigret Refuge's barrier beach, so information is limited on whether it is a key migration area.

Strategies:

■ Use the U.S. Shorebird Conservation Plan (once completed) to update management and monitoring strategies based on any newly identified imperiled species (draft Shorebird Prioritization System 1999).

■ By 2005, determine if there are key staging areas on the refuge. If so, map in a GIS database.

■ By 2006, determine potential threats and disturbances for key areas and implement a plan to reduce their impact. Use outreach and education and, if necessary, restrictions on public use and access.

Objective 1.9
Within 15 years of CCP completion, evaluate whether refuge lands can contribute to the recovery of the northeastern tiger beetle through reintroduction efforts initiated by the Service's Ecological Services Division, New England Field Office.

Background:
A Recovery Plan for the Northeastern Beach Tiger Beetle (*Cicindela dorsalis dorsalis*) was completed in September 1994. This species, which was described in the early 1900's as occurring in "great swarms", along beaches from Martha's Vineyard to New Jersey, is now only known in the northeast at two sites in Massachusetts. This beetle has been extirpated from the rest of Massachusetts, and all of Rhode Island, Connecticut, New York (Long Island) and New Jersey. This beetle is very vulnerable to disturbance while in its larval stage, which lasts two years. The larvae live in vertical burrows, generally in the beach intertidal zone, where they are sensitive to destruction by high levels of pedestrian traffic, vehicles, and other factors which alter the beach dynamic such as coastal development and beach stabilization structures. Population growth seems to be hampered by a lack of both undisturbed beaches and of nearby populations to provide a source for colonizing new sites.

Several sites in Rhode Island were identified as historic and extant sites for this beetle in the recovery plan, and, while subject to change, their future restoration and reintroduction potential was also identified. Sites for Rhode Island include Napatree Point (low-medium potential), Block Island (low potential), Narragansett Pier (low to no potential), Roger Williams Park (low to no potential), and Newport (low to no potential). While not specifically mentioned, Ninigret Refuge lies in proximity to Napatree Point and when considered together with the Ninigret Conservation Area, it may offer some future restoration potential.

Strategies:

■ By 2015, coordinate with the New England Field Office and RI DEM to determine the feasibility of reintroducing the beetles on the Rhode Island Refuge Complex or elsewhere along the South Shore of Rhode Island.

■ By 2016, develop site management and monitoring plans for prospective reintroduction sites on the Refuge Complex.

Objective 1.10
Promote an appreciation of amphibian and reptile conservation, and actively manage to protect and sustain current populations on the refuge.

Background:
Recent studies conducted by the University of RI have revealed that Ninigret and Trustom Pond refuges are very important to the reptile and amphibian population in the South County area. In fact, the highest density of two amphibian species known for Rhode Island occurs on these refuges. Unfortunately, we know little about how these amphibians and reptiles utilize refuge habitats seasonally, in particular during the spring amphibian migrations. Many of them appear to be relying on vernal pools, which are seasonal wetlands in forested habitat that fill with water during fall and spring; critical times in the life cycle of many frogs, toads, and salamanders. In cooperation with the University of RI, we hope to continue inventories at Trustom Pond and Ninigret refuges to gain information that will allow for more informed management decisions.

Strategies:

■ By 2003, conduct annual anuran call counts according to Regional protocol.

■ By 2005, develop environmental education and interpretation programs to promote the significance of the Complex to Rhode Island's herptofauna.

■ By 2005, work with conservation partners, RI DEM, The Friends Group, and volunteers to identify opportunities to reduce amphibian and reptile road mortality during spring migration.

■ By 2005, evaluate and incorporate recommendations (pending) made by Partners for Amphibian and Reptile Conservation (PARC) into refuge management, as warranted.

■ By 2005, implement a monitoring plan for the reptile and amphibian concentration areas identified in the University of RI study.

Objective 1.11
Protect, restore, and sustain rare plant sites on the refuge.

Background:

The Service has established new policy which provides guidance for maintaining and restoring, where appropriate, the biological integrity, diversity, and environmental health of refuges (FWS Manual, Chapter 3, part 601). One goal of the policy is to prevent the further loss of natural biological features and natural processes on refuges and within their respective landscapes. Included in this goal is the focus on sustaining native species and natural communities, such as those found under historic conditions, including single plant species or communities that may now be rare. Currently known on the refuge is a unique rare plant site containing six species the State considers rare or endangered. These include colic root, slimspike three-awn, yellow-fringed orchid, tall- and few-flowered nutrushes, and Indiangrass. As described in Chapter 3, this unique assemblage was studied by Killingbeck et al., although more work is needed to fully understand the dynamics at this site.

Strategies:

- By 2005, develop, with partners, a management, inventory, and monitoring plan for the yellow orchid and other rare plants site. Establish desired vegetation structure and composition, deer control, vegetation treatment methods (e.g. mechanical, prescribed fire, etc), and additional research needs.

- By 2008, with the Service's New England Field Office, RI DEM, and other partners, assess the potential for establishing or restoring Federal and State-listed species such as seabeach amaranth, sandplain gerardia, bushy rockrose, New England blazing star, and other former candidate plant species with potential habitat on the refuge.

Goal 2: Maintain and/or restore natural ecological communities to promote healthy, functioning ecosystems.

Objective 2.1

Within three years of CCP completion, design and implement a baseline inventory on refuge lands to determine the occurrence of species and habitats of management concern (Appendix A), and to serve as a basis for future management decisions.

Background:

To keep the HMP relevant, we will need to improve our general knowledge of important refuge resources, including their presence, distribution, and condition, to insure management actions are geared toward sustaining biological integrity, biological diversity, and ecosystem health as required by Service policy (FWS Manual, Chapter 3, part 601).

As stated in the introduction for this chapter, a Species and Habitat Inventory and Monitoring Plan will be completed in 2004. The following strategies will be incorporated into this plan.

Strategies:

- By 2004, develop a priority list of baseline biological inventory needs to better understand and document the biodiversity of the Refuge Complex, especially the presence and distribution of species and habitat types listed in Appendix A. Incorporate priorities into the HMP.

■ In 2004, begin inventories on the highest priority projects, incorporating the results into the CENSUS database, or other regional databases with GIS capabilities, to facilitate future analyses. Revise digital cover type maps as warranted.

Objective 2.2
Within 15 years of CCP implementation, maintain at least 220 acres as native, coastal sandplain grassland and shrubland (< 60 years old) to provide nesting habitat for landbirds of conservation concern such as bobolink, eastern meadowlark, and yellow-breasted chat.

Background:
Refuge staff are actively involved in restoring native, coastal sandplain grassland and shrubland (< 60 years old) on the refuge. We are managing to restore native vegetative structure and composition and to maintain the natural physical components and processes associated with a coastal sandplain community. Since current habitat conditions are highly altered from historic conditions, continuous evaluation of project effectiveness and an adaptive management response is imperative. All actively restored habitat areas are at least in 40 acre patches. Ideally, we are working towards contiguous areas of 100 acres or larger to provide the greatest benefit to the widest diversity of grassland and shrubland dependent species.

With the 220 acres targeted, we expect to increase nesting habitat for bobolinks, yellow breasted chat, and eastern meadowlarks. Less likely, but very desirable, would be sustained nesting by grassland bird species which require larger habitat patches, such as upland sandpipers and grasshopper sparrows.

Desired native coastal grassland plant species include, but are not limited to: little bluestem (*Schizachyrium scoparium*), big bluestem (*Andropogon gerardii*), Indian grass (*Sorghastrum nutans*), switchgrass (*Panicum virgatum*), common hairgrass (*Deshampsia flexuosa*), poverty-grass (*Danthonia spicata*), Pennsylvanian sedge (*Carex pennsylvanica*), rush (*Juncus greenei*), wild indigo (*Baptisia tinctoria*), native asters (*Aster* spp.), goldenrods (*Solidago* spp.), butterfly weed (*Asclepias tuberosa*), and dewberry (*Rubus hispidis* and *R. flagellaris*).

Desired native shrub species include, but are not limited to: northern arrowwood (*Viburnum dentatum*), sumacs (*Rhus spp*), bayberry (*Myrica pensylvanica*), high bush blueberry (*Vaccinium corymbosum*), and shadbush (*Amelanchier canadensis*).

Treatments to maintain these habitats includes the use of mechanical, prescribed fire, biological, and chemical herbicide treatments. All prescribed fires adhere to stipulations in the 1995 Fire EA. Mechanical treatments include brush hogging or hydroaxing woody vegetation, and discing, harrowing, plowing, packing, and drilling grassland fields. All herbicides used are on an approved Service list, and their use on the refuge is approved annually by the Regional Environmental Contaminants Specialist.

Strategies:

- Continue to implement the 1997 Environmental Assessment: Habitat Restoration Project, Ninigret NWR. The primary objective in the EA was to convert 70 acres of asphalt runway to native, early successional habitat. Strategies include use of mechanical manipulation (primarily brush hogging or hydroaxing woody vegetation, and discing, harrowing, plowing, packing, and drilling grassland fields), prescribed fire, biological controls, and chemical herbicide treatments.

- Continue to manipulate an additional 150 acres of adjacent older shrublands and juniper trees to create a mosaic of early successional (< 60 year old) shrublands and grasslands.

- By 2004, secure funding to complete principle restoration work on the 220 acre combined project area, and develop a maintenance and monitoring schedule for the project. All treatments will be consistent with the HMP.

- By 2005, hire a second maintenance worker for the Refuge Complex to implement the habitat restoration programs for the refuges.

- By 2010, evaluate restoration acres for potential regal fritillary butterfly sites in consultation with the Service's Ecological Services Division.

- By 2015, 85% of the 220-acre restoration project should be dominated (% cover) by native, early successional (< 60 year old) shrubland and grassland habitats, with invasive species dominating less than 15% of the area. Target native species are identified above.

Objective 2.3
Augment refuge restoration projects and contribute to regional conservation efforts by promoting shrubland and grassland habitat management on private lands.

Background:
Native grasslands and shrublands (< 60 years old), and those species dependent on them, are a concern because they are dramatically declining throughout the Northeast, especially large contiguous grasslands over 100 acres. The Refuge Complex offers relatively few areas on which to maintain large expanses of these habitats. As such, cooperative management on adjacent ownerships enhances the restoration work on the refuge by creating a larger habitat complex for area-sensitive native species.

Strategies:

- Maintain the habitat restoration sign at the Ninigret Refuge trailhead as an outreach tool.

- By 2005, establish a native habitat demonstration area on the refuge. Develop exhibits at the new Visitor Center, and conduct interpretive programs using volunteers and staff.

- By 2008, implement a "cooperative extension" outreach program and develop materials to provide technical support for interested landowners and conservation partners. The program may also include on-the-ground assistance.

Objective 2.4
Increase protection and restoration of beach strand habitats on the refuge, and promote their protection throughout South Shore communities.

Background:
Beach strand (also known as barrier beach) is one of the most imperiled habitat types on or adjacent to the refuges because of the combined impacts of development and recreation. Many species associated with this habitat type are either Federal or State-listed as threatened or endangered due to the associated impacts of human disturbance and habitat loss. Management of these areas is extremely complex and controversial, especially when it includes restrictions on beach use. Protection, restoration, and enhancement of beach strand habitat and dependent species was identified as the number one priority in the Connecticut River/Long Island Sound Ecosystem Team Plan (July 1996).

Strategies:

■ By 2003, in combination with piping plover outreach and education, promote increased protection and stewardship of beach strand habitat through an intensive outreach and education campaign with the Friends Group and other partners to target beach front landowners, elected officials, and beach visitors.

■ By 2003, hire two seasonal park aides to implement the project (same positions identified in Objective 1.4).

Objective 2.5
Restore natural conditions on 70 refuge acres to freshwater and tidal saltmarsh wetlands.

Background:
Wetlands are among the most productive ecosystems on earth, and salt marsh wetlands rank among the highest of wetlands, in terms of productivity. The tidal influence, including nutrient import, water abundance, and vegetative growth, all contribute to this productivity. Healthy wetlands function in ways that benefit the natural ecosystem and provide socio-economic values. Ecosystem values include the fact that certain fish, shellfish, birds, and mammals are wetland-dependent, spending their entire lives in these wetlands. Many waterfowl, wading birds, shorebirds, and other migratory birds utilize wetlands for feeding or resting, or to breed and raise their young. Wetlands are also essential habitats for many rare species of plants and animals. Wetlands function in ways that filter sediments and pollutants, produce oxygen, and support healthy microbiota for fish and wildlife. Socio-economic values include flood control, wave damage protection, hunting, trapping, fishing and shellfishing, aesthetics, education and research.

As noted in objective 1.7 above, maritime marsh is the habitat in most need of immediate conservation attention in this physiographic area due to the large number of priority species and the tremendous pressure from human development along the coastline. While we have identified restoration of only 70 acres on refuge lands, when coupled with the partnership effort described in objective 3.1, significant ecosystem and socio-economic benefits are expected.

The freshwater wetlands on the refuge also provide significant habitat for many species of concern. Objective 1.10 describes the importance of vernal pools to the diverse concentration of amphibians on the refuge. In addition to providing breeding habitat for amphibians, vernal pools support a food web rich in invertebrates favored by many birds, mammals, and reptiles.

Strategies:

■ By 2008, develop a plan to restore 70 wetland- acres on the refuge. Include consideration of the 1998 proposal by a former Refuge Biologist to restore wetlands (former vernal pools) discovered after removing the asphalt runways. In addition, evaluate all ditched and filled areas, including Hunters Island, to determine the feasibility of restoring natural hydrological flow through the refuge.

Objective 2.5
Within three years of CCP completion, treat at least 5 acres/year dominated by invasive, non-native plants on the refuge to (1) enhance native habitat, (2) eliminate new invasions, and (3) control the spread of established plants.

Background:
Issue 5 in Chapter 1 describes the implications of invasive plants on the refuges. These plants are a threat because they displace native plant and animal species, degrade wetlands and other natural communities, and reduce natural diversity and wildlife habitat values. They out-compete native species and can readily dominate a site. Early detection and consistent efforts at eradication are critical to maintain control over affected areas, or to prevent new invasions.

Strategies:

■ By 2004, identify and map the current distribution of non-native, invasive plant species on the refuge.

■ By 2005, prioritize treatment sites to prevent new invasions or eradicate recently established plants. Also of high priority are threatened, endangered, or rare plant sites or "pristine rare and exemplary vegetative communities" (March 1999 Invasive Plant Control Initiative, Strategic Plan for the Connecticut River Watershed/Long Island Sound).

■ By 2005, establish a program to treat an average of 5 acres/year of invasive, non-native species on the refuge using chemical, mechanical, prescribed fire and biological treatments as necessary. Strategies will be adapted based on monitoring and new information. A maintenance worker will be hired to administer treatments; this position will be shared among the other Rhode Island refuges.

Objective 2.6
Within 15 years of CCP completion, eliminate mute swan productivity from the refuge, and significantly reduce the presence of adults year round.

Background:
Non-native, invasive mute swan on the refuge adversely effect water quality on coastal ponds. Mute swan also impact our ability to maintain native biodiversity as they aggressively drive native waterfowl and shorebirds away from nesting sites, and compete with them for food.

Strategies:

■ In 2002, we will begin to implement the Service's policy (Memo FWS/MBMO/98-00043; based on Flyway Council recommendations) to prevent the establishment of, or to eliminate, mute swans. Strategies will be adapted as needed to pursue zero productivity of mute swans on the Refuge Complex. Each year, addling eggs will continue. Adult populations will be controlled using lethal and non-lethal techniques, particularly when habitat degradation is a concern, or if native species are displaced.

Objective 2.7
Within two years of CCP completion, develop a deer management plan for the Refuge Complex to address overabundant deer populations and evaluate recreational hunting opportunities.

Background:
Overabundant deer numbers are a concern on the refuge when they degrade habitat through excessive browsing or threaten human health and safety through increased vehicle collisions and incidences of Lyme disease. Since deer are highly mobile, it is difficult to effectively control a population unless they are managed throughout most or all of their range. The refuge has not closely monitored deer activities, including their impacts on refuge habitats. However, RI DEM has reported that complaints from citizens have increased in recent years about private property damage, worries of Lyme disease, vehicle collisions. RI DEM recommends hunting as the most effective tool to manage deer populations on the refuge.

Strategies:

■ In 2002, cooperate with RI DEM to develop a deer management plan and environmental assessment for the Refuge Complex. The plan will evaluate hunting to help manage deer numbers and provide a priority public use opportunity. A separate public involvement process will be initiated.

Map 41

Ninigret National Wildlife Refuge
Habitat Improvements
Comprehensive Conservation Plan

Legend:
- Grassland and Shrubland Habitat Management
- Wetland Restoration
- P Parking Lot
- Road or Street
- Barrier Free Trail
- Trail

Watchaug Pond

King Tom Pond

Post Road

Ninigret Park
(Town of Charlestown)

The Hummocks

Frosty Drew
Nature Center

Foster Cove

Hunter Island

Marshneck Point

Grassy Point

Coon Cove

Hall Point

RI

RI DEM Campground

Coop with stairs to restrict camping away from piping plover nesting habitat.

State restricts vehicles from beach during plover nesting season (April 1st - September 15th)

BLOCK ISLAND SOUND

Data Sources:

USGS 1:24,000 Roads & Hydrography
All other data provided by USFWS, RIGIS
& So. New England/NY Bight Coastal Program.

Map prepared for Rhode Island NWR Complex
Comprehensive Conservation Plan
June 2002
Refuge boundary has been modified for clarity.
Not to be used for legal purposes.

0   2000   4000   6000   Feet

0   600   1200   1800   Meters

N

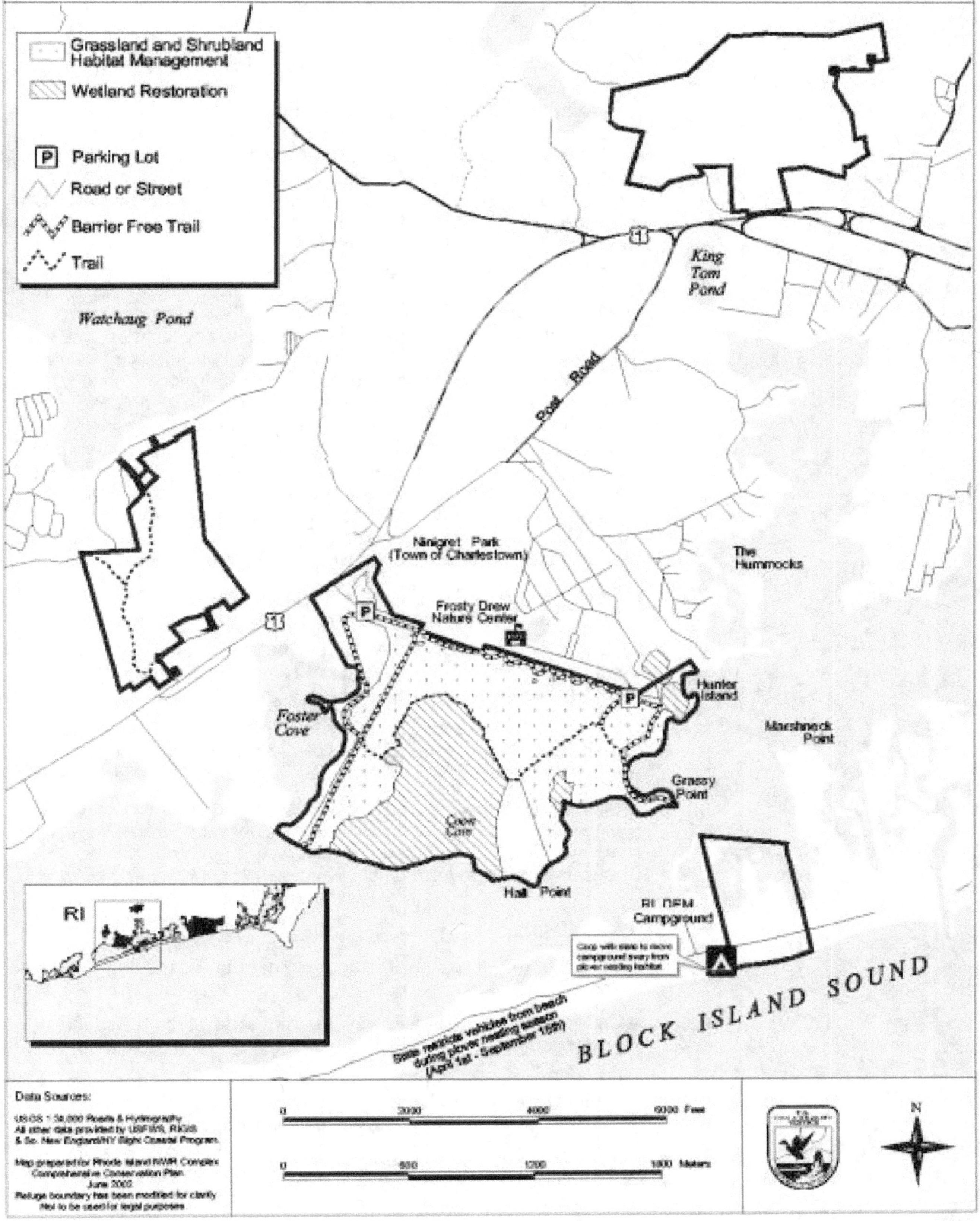

Goal 3: Establish a land protection program that fully supports accomplishment of species, habitat, and ecosystem goals.

Objective 3.1
Actively strive towards permanent protection of all trust resources at risk throughout southern Rhode Island.

Background:
Consistently mentioned in the PIF Area 9 Plan, the NAWMP, Joint Venture Plans, relevant Species Recovery Plans, and Ecosystem Plans is the need to protect, restore, and enhance additional high quality coastal habitats to contribute to the conservation of federal trust species. While land acquisition by the Service and other State, Federal, and local partners is a primary strategy for species conservation, each of these plans also recognizes the need to work in cooperation with private landowners to achieve conservation objectives. Technical and resource support, outreach, and education will all compliment land acquisition efforts.

The Draft CCP/EA (Chapter 3: Developing Land Protection Strategies) described our method of identifying acquisition lands of high conservation priority on Rhode Island's South Shore. During the planning process we determined that the Service is the logical leader in coastal land and water quality protection along the South Shore and on Block Island, with the existing refuges serving as anchors. Refuge expansions will significantly increase protection of the ecological values on current refuge lands, while also expanding protection and restoration of significant coastal habitats. We completed a Land Protection Plan for the Refuge Complex (Appendix E), which identifies specific tracts for Service acquisition. The LPP incorporates the following acquisition priorities:

■ Has documented occurrences of federally listed endangered or threatened species, or other priority federal trust resources;

■ Lies contiguous to existing refuge land, which could further enhance or protect the integrity of refuges by assembling the land base necessary to accomplish refuge goals;

■ Connects refuge land with other protected lands withing the South Shore and Block Island to help restore and promote the ecological integrity of the coastal wetland and beach strand complexes; and

■ Protects and sustains important natural communities that can be managed tin cooperation with other conservation partners in a manner that will contribute toward refuge goals and the conservation of federal trust resources.

Strategies:

■ Continue to assist conservation partners in identifying land protection needs, opportunities, and priorities in southern RI.

■ Continue to help partners seek funding sources for their land protection programs.

■ Beginning in 2002, expand the refuge acquisition boundary for Ninigret Refuge by the acres approved in the Land Protection Plan (LPP; Appendix E). Initiate acquisition from willing sellers, in either fee purchase or conservation easement, of 390 acres of high quality habitat.

Goal 4: Provide opportunities for high quality, compatible, wildlife-dependent public use with particular emphasis on environmental education and interpretation.

Integral to all of our public use objectives is development of a Visitor Services Plan in 2004 for the Refuge Complex. This plan will provide a coordinated strategy for implementing quality visitor services programs. We will emphasize the following six priority, wildlife-dependent uses identified in the 1997 Refuge Improvement Act where they are compatible with protecting wildlife resources: hunting, fishing, wildlife observation and photography, and environmental education and interpretation. The Visitor Service's Plan will also accomplish the following:

- Establish strategic goals and priorities for Visitor Services across the Refuge Complex;

- Identify target audiences and partnership opportunities for each refuge;

- Establish a methodology for determining visitor numbers, capacity limits, limits on visitor impacts to wildlife and habitats, and a means for assessing quality of visitor experiences;

- Evaluate recreational fee opportunities; and

- Establish an implementation schedule for priority Visitor Service's projects.

We will hire four outdoor recreation planners to implement the Visitor Services Plan and staff the planned Refuge Complex Visitor Center (see Chapter 5- Staffing). As new lands are acquired, opportunities to provide compatible, priority public uses will be pursued, following guidance in the Pre-acquisition Compatibility Determination (Appendix D).

The objectives below are designed to enhance existing, compatible, wildlife-dependent activities.

Objective 4.1
Provide high quality fishing opportunities along the refuge shoreline, while minimizing impacts to natural resources.

Strategies:

- Continue to allow surf fishing on the refuge's barrier beach, with vehicle access seasonally restricted from April 1 to September 15, which represents the nesting and migration seasons for piping plover and other shorebirds.

- Continue to support RI DEM's annual vehicle closure of the adjacent Ninigret Conservation Area beach from April 1 to September 15. Other access restrictions may be imposed if nesting piping plovers are found.

- Continue to allow recreational fishing from the shoreline and access to recreational and commercial shell fishing in Ninigret Pond, under State and refuge regulations, with access by foot only across the refuge to the pond.

- In 2003, designate and maintain access trails for shoreline fishing at Ninigret Pond to minimize impacts on habitat. Actively enforce use of trails.

■ In 2003, require commercial shell fishermen to have a refuge special use permit to allow better documentation of use and impacts.

Objective 4.2
Increase opportunities for high quality interpretive experiences on the refuge, which raise visitors awareness of the Refuge System and Ninigret Refuge's particular contribution to protecting trust resources and significant habitats.

Strategies:

■ Continue to maintain the two existing kiosks, updating information to keep it relevant and current.

■ Continue to use volunteers to assist in conducting interpretive programs.

■ Continue to participate in local Chamber of Commerce events, especially those conducted on the adjacent Ninigret Town Park.

■ By 2005, develop an interpretive program tiered to the Visitor Services Plan. Evaluate needs for new pamphlets, including a self-guided interpretive pamphlet, trail maps, and interpretive signs at the one current and two proposed barrier-free observation platforms.

■ By 2005, develop watchable wildlife literature and a species checklist.

■ By 2010, construct a visitor contact station, which will be seasonally staffed by volunteers or seasonal employees.

Objective 4.3
Improve opportunities for high quality wildlife observation and photography on the refuge, while minimizing impacts to natural resources.

Strategies:

■ Continue to allow access for these and other priority public use activities by means of foot travel, snowshoeing, cross country skiing, canoe or kayak.

■ Continue to annually maintain the existing wildlife observation platform at Grassy Point.

■ By 2003, secure funding to complete construction of the 3.8 mile "Trail Through Time." Public access will be restricted to the designated trail and shoreline access points.

■ By 2005, if determined feasible, construct up to two additional barrier-free observation platforms and/or viewing blinds at the grassland habitat restoration project area and/or in the Foster Cove area of Ninigret Pond.

Objective 4.4
Increase opportunities for high quality environmental educational experiences on the refuge, while minimizing impacts to natural resources.

Strategies:

■ Continue to allow Frosty Drew Nature Center to conduct environmental education trips on the refuge under a Memorandum of Agreement.

■ By 2003, annually sponsor at least one "Teach the Teacher" workshop as an effective way to reach many students and advocate protection and stewardship of natural resources.

■ By 2004, update the existing MOA with Frosty Drew to insure compatibility with the Visitor Services Plan. In addition, the for-profit program currently operating on the refuge will also be evaluated for its compatibility with other environmental education programs. If determined compatible, the for-profit group will be required to obtain a refuge special use permit.

■ By 2005, with partners, develop an environmental education program tiered to the Visitor Services Plan. We will establish two outdoor classroom sites featuring habitat restoration and salt pond ecology. We will pursue a volunteer environmental education corps to help with implementation on both Ninigret and Trustom Pond refuges.

Objective 4.5
Within two years of CCP completion, provide high quality waterfowl hunting opportunities on the refuge, and evaluate opportunities for deer hunting across the refuge.

Strategies:

■ In 2002, complete a deer management plan and environmental assessment evaluating opportunities for deer hunting. A separate public involvement process will be initiated. (Also refer to objective 2.7)

■ By 2003, develop Hunt Plan and fulfill other Service requirements to open the barrier beach portion of Ninigret Refuge to waterfowl hunting, including associated dog retrieval, for the fall 2003 season. Hunting will be administered according to state and local regulations, and will be by boat access only. Additional refuge regulations may be determined necessary during development of the Hunt Plan. The hunt program will be administered in cooperation with RI DEM.

■ Expand the waterfowl hunt area to include Coon Cove, for boat access only, when habitat conditions are restored (e.g. *Phragmites* is eliminated) such that the area provides a quality hunting opportunity.

Objective 4.6
Within three years of CCP completion, eliminate incompatible, non-wildlife dependent public uses on the refuge.

Background:
Incompatible, non-wildlife dependent activities detract from our ability to fulfill refuge purposes and often conflict with priority public uses. None of these uses are necessary for the safe, practical, or effective conduct of a priority public use, and in fact, are often disruptive to priority public uses. Limited refuge resources should not be expended to manage activities that do not contribute to the public's understanding and appreciation of the refuge's wildlife or cultural resources, or to activities that do not directly benefit these resources.

Strategies:

■ In 2003, phase out dog walking and bicycling. Walking dogs on leash and bicycling had previously been allowed on runways. Under the decision for the 1997 "Habitat Restoration Project EA: Ninigret Refuge", these uses were to be eliminated once the runways had been removed.

■ By 2004, increase resource protection and management of public use by utilizing law enforcement personnel to provide more consistent and thorough outreach and enforcement of refuge regulations. In particular, the following activities will be targeted on the refuge: roller blading, jogging, kite flying, swimming and sunbathing.

■ By 2004, hire at least one additional law enforcement officer to enforce refuge regulations for the Refuge Complex.

Goal 5: Provide refuge staffing, operations, and maintenance support to effectively accomplish refuge goals and objectives.

Staffing, operations, and maintenance needs are addressed in Chapter 5.

Map 4-2

Ninigret National Wildlife Refuge
Public Use
Comprehensive Conservation Plan

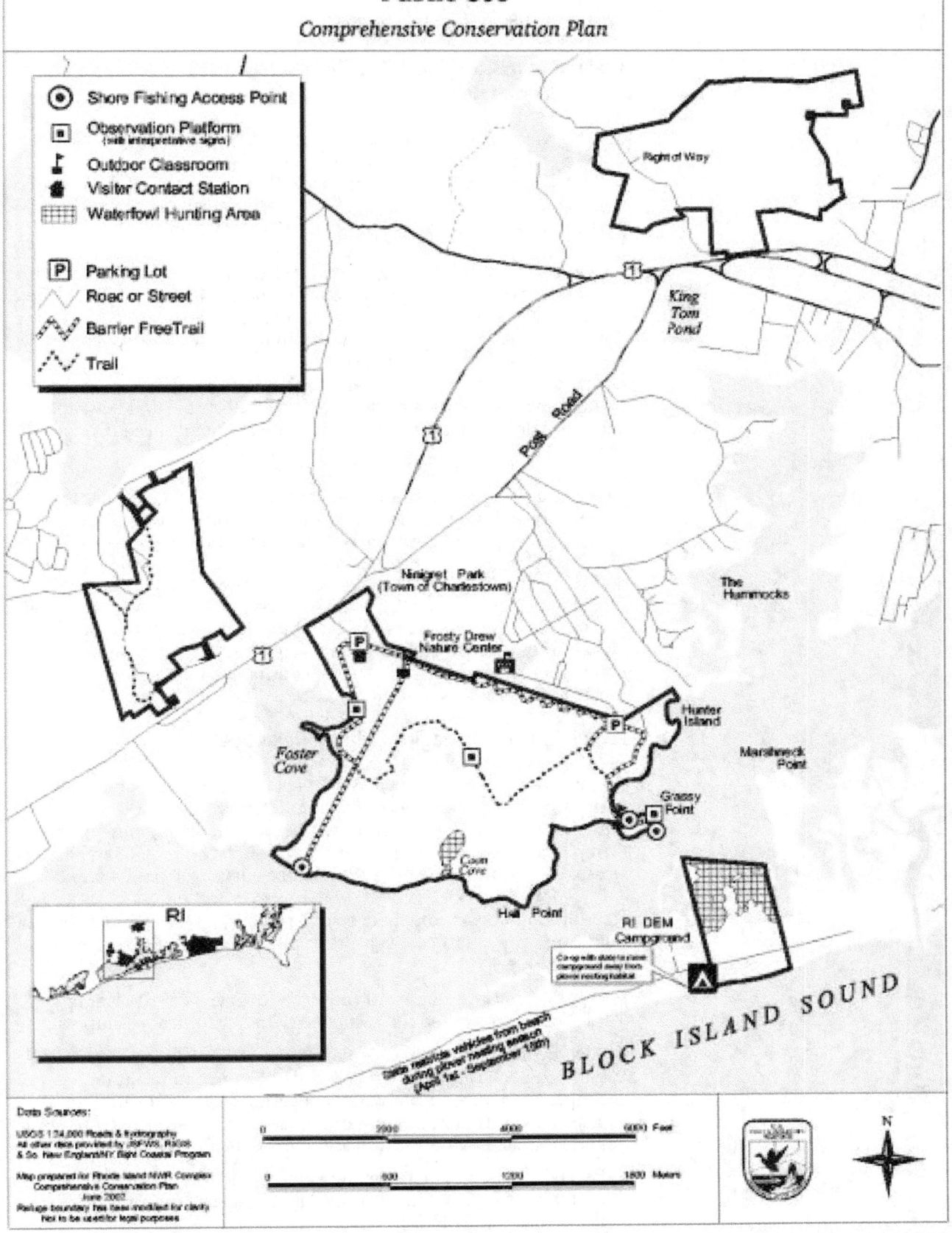

Legend:
- ⊙ Shore Fishing Access Point
- ▣ Observation Platform (with interpretative signs)
- Outdoor Classroom
- Visitor Contact Station
- Waterfowl Hunting Area
- P Parking Lot
- Road or Street
- Barrier Free Trail
- Trail

Right of Way

King Tom Pond

Post Road

Ninigret Park (Town of Charlestown)

The Hummocks

Frosty Drew Nature Center

Foster Cove

Hunter Island

Marshneck Point

Grassy Point

Coon Cove

Hall Point

RI DEM Campground

Co-op with state to move campground away from plover nesting habitat

RI

State restricts vehicles from beach during plover nesting season (April 1st - September 15th)

BLOCK ISLAND SOUND

Data Sources:

USGS 1:24,000 Roads & Hydrography
All other data provided by USFWS, RIGIS
& So. New England/NY Bight Coastal Program

Map prepared for Rhode Island NWR Complex
Comprehensive Conservation Plan
June 2002
Refuge boundary has been modified for clarity.
Not to be used for legal purposes.

0   2000   4000   6000 Feet

0   600   1200   1800 Meters

N

General Refuge Management Direction

The following management direction applies to all of the refuge goals and across all program areas. Some of this direction is required by Service policy or legal mandates.

Maintaining Biological Integrity, Diversity, and Environmental Health

The Service finalized its policy on Maintaining the Biological Integrity, Diversity, and Environmental Health of the National Wildlife Refuge System in January 2001 (FWS manual, Part 601, Chapter 3). This policy directs us, first and foremost, to maintain existing levels of biological integrity, diversity, and environmental health on refuges. Secondarily, we will restore lost or severely degraded elements of integrity, diversity, and environmental health on refuges where it is feasible and supports refuge purpose(s). To implement the policy on refuges, refuge managers are directed to determine: each refuge's relationship between refuge purpose(s) and biological integrity, diversity, and environmental health; what conditions constitute biological integrity, diversity, and environmental health; how to maintain existing levels of all three; and how, and when to appropriately restore lost elements of all three (Chapter 3, section 3.9)

The objectives and strategies laid out in this CCP generally improve the biological integrity, diversity, and environmental health of the refuge. Management actions emphasize maintaining current species and habitat diversity, recovering endangered and threatened species, and restoring natural ecosystem processes and functions. Implementation of the CCP will increase our understanding of the refuge's current resources, sustainable natural conditions, and the effects of our management actions. In addition, our strategy of adaptive management will provide continuous improvement toward meeting this policy's intent.

Protecting and Managing Cultural Resources

By law, we must consider the effects of our actions on archeological and historic resources. We will comply with Section 106 of the National Historic Preservation Act before disturbing any ground. Compliance may require any or all of the following: a State Historic Preservation Records survey, literature survey, or field survey.

In addition to basic compliance requirements, we will undertake the following projects to better protect and interpret cultural resources on the refuge:

- By 2005, initiate a cultural resources overview of the Refuge Complex to increase the available data on cultural resources.

- Also by 2005, develop a Memorandum of Understanding (MOU) with the Narragansett Indian Tribal Council to facilitate cooperation on environmental education and interpretation, to improve our understanding of the context of natural resources, and to increase site identification and protection.

- By 2006, train at least one law enforcement officer on the refuge in regulations associated with the Archeological Resources Protection Act (ARPA).

Tribal Coordination

Increasing communication with the Narragansett Indian Tribal Council is very important for the Refuge Complex. As noted above, we plan to develop an MOU by 2005 to establish a mutually beneficial working relationship that includes cooperating in environmental education and interpretation and protecting cultural resources.

Coastal Resources Management Council Coordination

The federal Coastal Zone Management Act (16 U.S.C. §1451, as amended) requires the Service to work with the State Coastal Resources Management Council (CRMC) to insure refuge programs and activities are consistent to the maximum extent practicable with the enforceable policies adopted by the state. The CRMC's concurrence with the Service's Federal Consistency Determination on the CCP was predicated on meeting the following management direction:

1) Provide Separate Consistency Determinations for Major Construction Projects. Major construction projects such as buildings, parking lots, roads, and boardwalks, which the Service determines may effect coastal resources, will require separate federal consistency determinations for each project.

2) Annual Coordination Meetings. Refuge Complex and CRMC staff will meet at least once annually to review general plans and projects which the Service has determined may effect coastal resources. These meetings will cover proposals for the forthcoming calendar year. The objective of these meetings will be to provide CRMC staff with available details on what is being proposed and to address their concerns. It is mutually understood that some projects may not be fully developed at the time of meeting.

Refuge Revenue Sharing Payments

Annual refuge revenue sharing payments to the Town of Charlestown will continue. Future increases in payments will be commensurate with increases in the appraised fair market values of refuge lands, new acquisitions of land, and new Congressional appropriations.

Contaminant Site Remediation

The obvious concerns with human health and safety, and impacts to wildlife from contaminants, requires timely and thorough remediation of contaminated sites. Refuge Complex staff will continue coordinating with the Environmental Protection Agency (EPA), Rhode Island Department of Environmental Management (RI DEM), Army Corps of Engineers (ACOE), or delegated authorities, to finalize remediation plans and begin cleaning up the four sites on Ninigret Refuge, collectively listed in the CERCLIS database as site No. RI91435302601.

Controlling Mosquitos

Within the past few years, incidences of mosquito-borne Eastern
Equine Encephalitis and West Nile virus have elevated public health
concerns about mosquito control in the Middle Atlantic States.
Mosquito control has been very limited on the Refuge Complex, and
has occurred only at the direct request of the State's Mosquito
Abatement Office. During the last 5 years, we used two very localized
applications of the larvicide Bti on two problem breeding sites. Our
Regional Contaminants Specialist pre-approved those applications.

In general, we will not use larvicides on the Refuge Complex to control
mosquitos. However, in cooperation with neighboring towns and the
Mosquito Abatement Office, we will consider applying larvicides on a
case-by-case basis, particularly when there is an elevated public health
risk. The Service is now evaluating this issue on a regional basis, and
has begun preparation for an environmental impact statement. This
may result in Service policy or Regional guidelines being developed
and incorporated into this CCP in the future.

Permitting Special Use (including Research)

Requests for special use permits will be evaluated by the Refuge
Manager on a case-by-case. All permitted activities must be
determined appropriate and compatible through a compatibility
determination. At a minimum, all commercial activities and all
research projects require a special use permit. Research projects that
will improve and strengthen natural resource management decisions
on the Refuge Complex will generally be approved. The Refuge
Manager will encourage partnerships with local universities and
colleges to facilitate research that will help evaluate CCP objectives
and strategies, or the assumptions on which they are based.

The Refuge Manager may also consider research not directly related
to refuge objectives, but which contributes to the broader
enhancement, protection, or management of native species and
biological diversity within the region.

Each refuge will maintain a list of research needs to provide
prospective researchers or organizations upon request. The Refuge
Manager will determine on a case-by-case basis whether they can
directly support a project through funding, in-kind services (e.g.
housing or use of other facilities), field assistance, or through sharing
data and records. Research results will be shared within the Service,
and with RI DEM.

All researchers on refuges, current and future, are required to submit a detailed research proposal following Service policy in the FWS Refuge Manual, Chapter 4 Section 6. Special use permits must also identify a schedule for progress reports (at least annual), criteria for determining when a project should cease, and publication or other final reporting requirements. The Regional Refuge Biologists, other Service divisions, and state agencies will be asked to review and comment on research proposals.

Some projects, such as depredation and banding studies, require additional Service permits. These projects will not be approved until all Service permits and Endangered Species Act consultation requirements are met. Also, to maintain the natural landscape of the refuge, projects which require permanent or semi-permanent structures will not be allowed, except for extenuating circumstances unforseen at this time.

Chapter 5

Indian grass
USFWS photo

Implementation and Monitoring

- Refuge Complex Staffing
- Refuge Complex Funding
- Step-down Management Plans
- Partnerships
- Volunteer Program
- Monitoring and Evaluation
- Adaptive Management
- Compatibility Determinations
- Additional NEPA Analysis
- Plan Amendment and Revision

Refuge Complex Staffing

The five Rhode Island Refuges are managed as a Refuge Complex, with centrally stationed staff taking on duties at multiple refuges. A total of 26 full time personnel, one Student-to-Career Experience Program (SCEP) trainee, and 17 seasonal personnel, are needed to fully implement all five Refuge CCPs. Permanent staff serving all five refuges may be stationed at the Refuge Headquarters in Charlestown, RI, or at Sachuest Point Refuge in Middletown, RI. Some permanent and temporary staff may be stationed seasonally on Block Island Refuge. Appendix G identifies currently filled positions, recommended new positions, and the overall supervisory structure. The new positions identified will increase visitor services, biological expertise, and visibility of the Service on refuge lands.

Refuge Complex Funding

Successful implementation of the CCPs for each refuge relies on our ability to secure funding, personnel, infrastructure, and other resources to accomplish the actions identified. Full implementation of the actions and strategies in all five Refuge Complex CCPs would incur one-time costs of $8.9 million. This includes staffing, major construction projects, and individual resource program expansions. Most of these projects have been identified as Tier 1 or Tier 2 Projects in the National Wildlife Refuge System's Refuge Operations Needs System database (RONS). Appendix F lists RONS projects and their recurring costs, such as salaries, following the first year. Also presented in Appendix F is a list of projects in the Service's current Maintenance Management System (MMS) database for the Refuge Complex. Currently, the MMS database lists $3.85 million in maintenance needs for the Refuge Complex.

Land acquisition costs are identified separately. The Land Protection Plan (LPP, Appendix E) expanded the Refuge Complex acquisition boundary by 2,681 acres, increasing the total unacquired acreage to 3,130. We estimate the value of these lands to be $83 million at current, fair-market prices. In all probability, the Refuge Complex will protect these lands at a lower cost, as some parcels may be protected through conservation easements or acquired through donation or land exchange.

Step-Down Management Plans

The Refuge System Manual (Part 4 Chapter 3) lists more than 25 Step-Down Management Plans generally required on most refuges. Step-down plans describe specific management actions a refuge will follow to achieve objectives or implement management strategies. Some require annual revision, others are revised on a 5- to 10-year schedule. Some require additional NEPA analysis, public involvement, and compatibility determinations before they can be implemented. A status list of Rhode Island Refuge Complex step-down plans follows.

These plans are current :

■ Fire Management Plan, 1995 (Refuge Complex); updated with annual burn plans

■ Grasslands Management Plan, 1994 (Trustom Pond Refuge); will be incorporated into the Habitat Management Plan for the Refuge Complex in 2003

■ Continuity of Operations Plan, 1998 (Refuge Complex)

■ Animal Control Plan, 1995 (Refuge Complex); will be updated with Integrated Predator Management and Trapping Plans for the Refuge Complex

These plans are now in draft form or being prepared:

■ Safety Program and Operations Plan (Refuge Complex)

■ Law Enforcement Plan (Refuge Complex)

These plans exist, but we consider them out-of-date and needing revisions as indicated:

■ Water Management Plan (Trustom Pond Refuge); incorporate into Habitat Management Plan by 2003

■ Hunting Plan (Trustom Pond Refuge); incorporate into Hunt Plan for the Refuge Complex in 2003

■ Sign Plan (Refuge Complex); expand to Facilities and Sign Plan by 2005

■ Croplands Management Plan (Trustom Pond Refuge); incorporate into Habitat Management Plan for Refuge Complex in 2003

These step-down plans need to be initiated and will be completed by the indicated dates:

■ Refuge Complex Habitat Management Plan (highest priority step down plan) in 2003

■ Refuge Complex Hunt Plan in 2003

■ Refuge Complex Species and Habitat Inventory and Monitoring Plan in 2004

■ Integrated Predator Management Plan in 2004

■ Refuge Complex Visitor Services Plan in 2004

■ Fishing Plan by 2005

■ Trapping Plan by 2004

Partnerships

The Refuge Complex staff is proud of its long history of partnerships. More than 45 partnerships have supported the refuges, including four universities and colleges, numerous departments within Rhode Island State government, town administrations, conservation commissions, school districts, conservation groups and land trusts, environmental education centers, historic preservation groups, adjacent landowners, and other federal agencies. These partnerships have resulted in biological research, cooperative management of threatened and endangered species and declining habitats, protection of open space, and environmental education programs.

Refuge staff were particularly delighted by the establishment in 1998 of a "Friends of the National Wildlife Refuges of Rhode Island" group. The Friends are a non-profit advocacy group dedicated to supporting Refuge Complex goals within the community through public education and interpretation, project funding, and volunteer coordination. Their mission is "...[to be] devoted to the conservation and development of needed healthy habitat for flora and fauna at the National Wildlife Refuges of Rhode Island and to the provision of a safe, accessible ecological experience for our visitors...."

We will strengthen and formalize refuge partnerships to promote coordinated management and facilitate sharing of resources. Our partnership with the Friends Group is vitally important to us for community relations and for support in implementing our resource programs. Partnerships help us build support for the refuge, facilitate the sharing of information, and supplement the efforts of refuge staff.

Strategies:
- By 2003, we will conduct at least semi-annual meetings with the Friends Group to promote communication and evaluate implementation of the MOU. We will continue to actively support and promote the Friends Group's vital efforts in funding and implementing outreach and environmental education programs, which enhance our ability to meet refuge goals.

- By 2005, develop formal agreements with current partners, such as the South County Tourism Council, local land trusts, and conservation organizations, to identify mutual goals, and opportunities for cost sharing, technical exchange and environmental education and interpretation.

Volunteer Program

Volunteers are vital to accomplishing all Refuge Complex goals. For example, in fiscal years 2000 and 2001, volunteers donated 9,332 and 10,000 hours respectively, assisting in environmental education programs, monitoring public use, maintaining facilities, and managing habitats. This translates to more than $110,000 worth of services contributed to the refuges in 2000 and $117,900 in 2001. Volunteers are also largely responsible for staffing the visitor contact station at Trustom Pond Refuge.

In 1999 we hired a permanent staff Volunteer Coordinator to improve the quality of the program through better coordination, supervision and training of volunteers, and to better integrate volunteers into all refuge programs. The coordinator compiles and distributes a quarterly newsletter to volunteers, refuge partners, and interest groups, keeping them informed about management activities and upcoming interpretive programs on the Refuge Complex.

Maintaining Existing Facilities

Periodic maintenance of existing facilities is critical to ensure safety and accessibility for Refuge Complex staff and visitors. Existing facilities include the Trustom Pond Refuge visitor contact station, Refuge Complex maintenance compound, and numerous parking areas, observation platforms, and trails. Many of these facilities are not currently Americans With Disabilities Act (ADA) compliant; upgrading is needed. Appendix F displays the fiscal year (FY) 2000 Maintenance Management System (MMS) database list of backlogged maintenance entries for the Refuge Complex.

We will also undertake the following strategies to improve the visibility of the Service:

- By 2003, meet with RI DOT to modify existing U.S. Route 1 directional signs. At a minimum, propose changes to the existing sign directing visitors "To Moonstone Beach".
- By 2005, complete construction of the Visitor Center/Headquarters for the Refuge Complex, implementing recommendations for interior facility design from the August 1999 Project Identification Document. At least one Visitor Services Specialist will be hired to administer the new facility.
- By 2005, complete a Refuge Complex Facilities and Sign Plan.

Monitoring and Evaluation

Monitoring and evaluation for this CCP will occur at two levels. The first level, which we refer to as implementation monitoring, responds to the question, "Did we do what we said we would do, when we said we would do it?" Annual implementation monitoring will be achieved by using the checklist in Appendix H for the Refuge Complex.

The second level of monitoring, which we refer to as effectiveness monitoring, responds to the question, "Are the actions we proposed effective in achieving the results we had hoped for?" Or, in other words, "Are the actions leading us toward our vision, goals, and objectives?" Effectiveness monitoring evaluates an individual action, a suite of actions, or an entire resource program. This approach is more analytical in evaluating management effects on species, populations, habitats, refuge visitors, ecosystem integrity, or the socio-economic environment. More often, the criteria to monitor and evaluate these management effects will be established in step-down, individual project, or cooperator plans, or through the research program. The Species and Habitat Inventory and Monitoring Plan, to be completed in 2004, will be based on the needs and priorities identified in the Habitat Management Plan.

Adaptive Management

This CCP is a dynamic document. A strategy of adaptive management will keep it relevant and current. Through scientific research, inventories and monitoring, and our management experiences, we will gain new information which may alter our course of action. We acknowledge that our information on species, habitats, and ecosystems is incomplete, provisional, and subject to change as our knowledge base improves.

Objectives and strategies must be adaptable in responding to new information and spatial and temporal changes. We will continually evaluate management actions, through monitoring or research, to reconsider whether their original assumptions and predictions are still valid. In this way, management becomes an active process of learning "what really works". It is important that the public understand and appreciate the adaptive nature of natural resource management.

The Refuge Manager is responsible for changing management actions or objectives if they do not produce the desired conditions. Significant changes may warrant additional NEPA analysis; minor changes will not, but will be documented in annual monitoring, project evaluation reports, or the annual refuge narratives.

Compatibility Determinations

Federal law and policy provide the direction and planning framework to protect the Refuge System from incompatible or harmful human activities and to insure that Americans can enjoy Refuge System lands and waters. The National Wildlife Refuge System Administration Act of 1966, as amended by the National Wildlife Refuge System Improvement Act of 1997, is the key legislation on managing public uses and compatibility.

Before activities or uses are allowed on a National Wildlife Refuge, we must determine that each is a "compatible use." A compatible use is a use that, based on the sound professional judgement of the Refuge Manager, " ...will not materially interfere with or detract from the fulfillment of the mission of the Refuge System or the purposes of the refuge." "Wildlife-dependent recreational uses may be authorized on a refuge when they are compatible and not inconsistent with public safety. Except for consideration of consistency with State laws and regulations as provided for in section (m), no other determinations or findings are required to be made by the refuge official under this Act or the Refuge Recreation Act for wildlife-dependent recreation to occur." (Refuge Improvement Act)

Compatibility determinations were distributed (in the draft CCP/EA) for a 51 day public review in early 2001. These determinations have since been approved, and will allow the continuation of the following public use programs: wildlife observation and photography, environmental education and interpretation, fishing, and hunting. A pre-acquisition compatibility determination was also reviewed and completed, and identifies which existing public uses would be allowed to continue on new properties acquired by the Refuge complex. Since releasing the draft CCP/EA, we have also distributed compatibility determinations for trapping and waterfowl hunting for a public review period. All comments were considered and utilized in the revision. These new compatibility determinations are now final and included in Appendix D.

Additional compatibility determinations will be developed when appropriate new uses are proposed. Compatibility determinations will be re-evaluated by the Refuge Manager when conditions under which the use is permitted change significantly; when there is significant new information on effects of the use; or at least every 10 years for non-priority public uses. Priority public use compatibility determinations will be re-evaluated under the conditions noted above, or at least every 15 years with revision of the CCP. Additional detail on the compatibility determination process is in Parts 25, 26, and 29 of Title 50 of the Code of Federal Regulations, effective November 17, 2000.

Additional NEPA Analysis

The National Environmental Policy Act (NEPA) requires a site-specific analysis of impacts for all federal actions. These impacts are to be disclosed in either an EA or Environmental Impact Statement (EIS).

Most of the actions and associated impacts in this plan were described in enough detail in the draft CCP/EA to comply with NEPA, and will not require additional environmental analysis. Although this is not an all-inclusive list, the following programs are examples that fall into this category: protecting piping plover, restoring area-defined grasslands and wetlands, implementing priority wildlife-dependent public use programs (except deer hunting), acquiring land, and controlling invasive plants.

Other actions are not described in enough detail to comply with the site-specific analysis requirements of NEPA. Examples of actions that will require a separate EA include: construction of a new visitor center and headquarters, new deer hunting opportunities, and future habitat restoration projects not fully developed or delineated in this document. Monitoring, evaluation, and research can generally be increased without additional NEPA analysis.

Plan Amendment and Revision

Periodic review of the CCP will be required to ensure that objectives are being met and management actions are being implemented. Ongoing monitoring and evaluation will be an important part of this process. Monitoring results or new information may indicate the need to change our strategies.

The Service's planning policy (FWS Manual, Part 602, Chapters 1, 3, and 4) states that CCPs should be reviewed at least annually to decide if they require any revisions (Chapter 3, part 3.4 (8)). Revisions will be necessary if significant new information becomes available, ecological conditions change, major refuge expansions occur, or when we identify the need to do so during a program review. At a minimum, CCPs will be fully revised every 15 years. We will modify the CCP documents and associated management activities as needed, following the procedures outlined in Service policy and NEPA requirements. Minor revisions that meet the criteria for categorical exclusions (550 FW 3.3C) will only require an Environmental Action Statement.

www.ingramcontent.com/pod-product-compliance
Lightning Source LLC
Chambersburg PA
CBHW080514290526
45790CB00006B/2169